𝔚illiams 𝔠ollege
DAVID A. WELLS PRIZE ESSAYS

𝔑umber 3

Smuggling
in the
American Colonies
at the
Outbreak of the Revolution

with
Special Reference to the West Indies Trade

William S. McClellan

HERITAGE BOOKS
2007

HERITAGE BOOKS

AN IMPRINT OF HERITAGE BOOKS, INC.

Books, CDs, and more—Worldwide

For our listing of thousands of titles see our website
at
www.HeritageBooks.com

A Facsimile Reprint
Published 2007 by
HERITAGE BOOKS, INC.
Publishing Division
65 East Main Street
Westminster, Maryland 21157-5026

Originally Printed for the
Department of Political Science of Williams College

New York
Moffat, Yard and Company
1912

International Standard Book Number: 978-0-7884-0639-3

SMUGGLING IN THE AMERICAN COLONIES AT THE OUTBREAK OF THE REVOLUTION

WITH

SPECIAL REFERENCE TO THE WEST INDIES TRADE

PREFACE

THE importance of whatever economic and governmental questions are involved in a study of smuggling at the outbreak of the American Revolution consists primarily in the relation they bear to the larger questions of a similar nature, operative at the time. In general terms, the Revolution was the result of a constantly developing spirit of independence, into which entered many elements, the political being quite as important as the economic. It will be the purpose of this essay, then, to establish the particular function which smuggling—and especially that in connection with the West Indies trade—performed in bringing to bear the influences exerted by these two elements. To accomplish this it is essential to treat of the development of American colonial trade and with it the growth and operation of the British commercial and colonial systems, in which are found both causes and effects of the prevalence of smuggling.

The endeavor has been made to eliminate from this essay the many features of the British colonial and commercial systems which do not have a very direct bearing on the question of smuggling, but it has seemed necessary to show cause why many of these features are without special significance in a discussion of the economic and governmental questions which arise. No attempt has been made to assign any comparative rating to the influence which smuggling may have had among the forces which resulted in the Revolution.

Due reference has been made in the footnotes to the source material and secondary authorities consulted, while, for convenience, a complete list of such works has been appended. The writer is greatly indebted to Assistant Professor David Taggart Clark of Williams College for assistance in the preparation of the manuscript for publication.

WILLIAM SMITH McCLELLAN.

YORK, PA., October, 1912.

CONTENTS

CHAPTER I

CHAPTER II

CHAPTER III

CHAPTER IV

CHAPTER V

INTRODUCTION

This is the third in the Williams series of
David A. Wells prize essays in Political
Science. In 1904 Mr. Elwin L. Page was
awarded the prize for an essay on "The Con-
tributions of the Landed Man to Civil
Liberty;" in 1907 Mr. Shepard A. Morgan
for an essay on "The History of Parliamentary Taxation in England." Mr. McClellan
received the prize for the essay following, in
1911.

The competition is open to Seniors in
Williams College, and to graduates of not
more than three years' standing. As Williams
offers no graduate courses it is obvious, under
these circumstances, that the award does not
demand original research, but calls rather for
"evidences of careful reading of secondary
authorities," and the "thoughtful handling"
and working over of material readily acces-
sible upon the subjects from time to time
suggested for treatment.

In the present essay Mr. McClellan follows Professor Ashley and others in carefully and justly distinguishing between the general body of restrictive trade laws constituting the old English "colonial system," and the special protective legislation of 1733 passed in the single interest of the sugar-planters of the British West Indies, the famous "Molasses Act." The former, the general restrictive laws, the author holds, did not operate as serious actual constraint, since England, the legal beneficiary, was the natural monopolist of the colonial trade; the latter, the "Molasses Act," defied the natural channels of commerce.

As a result of these circumstances, the violations of the general "system" were probably, the essayist writes, relatively slight and unimportant, but the restrictions on imports from the West Indies were systematically and persistently ignored, producing a condition of smuggling so universal and well-nigh respectable as to raise the question whether the operations of the merchants could properly be designated by that term.

When a reforming British minister, at the

end of the French and Indian War, sought to "clean up" America in this regard, while he tried to induce the colonists to pay a minor share of the expenses of their own defence, though he reduced the molasses duties by half almost as soon as he tried to collect them, his zeal for fiscal efficiency proved both futile and ill-timed. Otis had already quickened the spirit of protest against administrative surveillance, and now commercial irritation at interference with established courses became blended with repugnance to outside taxation of any sort, and ultimately lost in the larger political issue of the complete realization of the spirit, innate in the colonies, of American independence. Such is the very briefest outline of Mr. McClellan's essay.

Thus the author shows again the error in the idea that the colonists fought the Revolution simply in order to free themselves from the general constraint of the colonial system, while he makes clear the force and meaning of the admission which John Adams declared himself unashamed to make "that molasses was an essential ingredient of our independence."

Chapters III and V, containing the bulk of the author's distinctive material, and his conclusions, or better Chapters III to the end, may be especially commended to the busy reader, but the short introductory chapter on the New World commerce, and the well-summarized account of "The English Commercial System" in Chapter II, appropriately introduce the main subject of the essay, which may well be read entire for the interesting and important testimony, from contemporary and later writers, which the author has co-ordinated together on the commercial life of our great-great-grandfathers, and on the relations of economic and political forces to the birth of the American Republic.

The subject set for competition having been "Smuggling in the American Colonies at the Outbreak of the Revolution with especial Reference to the West Indies Trade," Mr. McClellan did not attempt to go at length into the somewhat controverted question of the amount of violation of the general Trade Acts, particularly of the great Statute of 1663 which sought to confine so much of the colonial import trade to England. I incline to the opinion that a more thorough investigation of all the evidence available on this question than has yet, so far as I am aware, been made might show somewhat greater prevalence of the smuggling in of European goods than the author's essay, in its present form at any rate, and some of the authorities, concede. The future works to come from the authoritative hand of Mr. Beer will undoubtedly illumine this question. I incline to think, also, that the "enumeration" of great colonial exports operated at times and in places as a slightly more conscious inconvenience than has sometimes been suggested.

Mr. McClellan was unfortunately deprived of the fullest opportunity which he would have desired, to work his essay over before publication.

Whatever the facts may have been before 1763 or before 1775, it seems indisputable that the time must before many years have come when the general restrictions of the colonial system, if unmodified, would have proved either an intolerable shackle upon American development, or else unenforceable, or more likely both. The priority of England in the great inventions and the distraction of the Continent in war would have postponed, but could hardly have averted the time. Had American commercial freedom not been obtained when it was, or before many decades, the wonderful story of material progress which ensued must have read some degrees less marvelously. The old English colonial system, like all other similar systems, was economically vicious, and unenlightenedly selfish, to the profit of a part and not of the whole, whatever the Navigations Acts may have done for New England shipping or British power on the sea. The very recent language of a French critic of his country's colonial policy states a principle as true in the past as now. "Ce n'est pas en réduisant le pouvoir d'achat des indigènes, en leur rendant l'existence plus difficile, et en augmentant les prix de revient de toutes les enterprises coloniales que l'on favorisera la mise en valeur de nos colonies et leur puissance de production, donc d'acquisition par voie d'échange".[1]

Happily for the British Empire, since the days of Grenville and Sheffield, England has

[1] Journ. des Économistes, févr., 1912, p. 227.

learned a wisdom that some rivals and some of
her own colonies might well emulate. Should
the day come of her relapse to bygone falla-
cies, she would deal with her own hand as
serious a blow as any that she might give to
her own enduring wealth and power.

By the terms of the foundation of the
competition, "No subject shall be selected
for competitive writing or investigating and
no essay shall be considered which in any way
advocates or defends the spoliation of property under form or process of law; or the
restriction of commerce in times of peace by
legislation, except for moral or sanitary purposes; or the enactment of usury laws; or
the impairment of contracts by the debase-
ment of coin; or the issue and use by Government of irredeemable notes or promises to
pay intended to be used as currency and as
a substitute for money; or which defends the
endowment of such 'paper,' 'notes,' and
'promises to pay' with the legal tender quality." A subject more congenial than the
present to the spirit and letter of this pro-
vision, or more appropriate could hardly be
found to commemorate the name and the

doctrine as an economist of the distinguished worker whose generosity established these prizes. A more striking or momentous instance of legislative favoritism and legislative fatuity can scarcely exist, in all the modern history of blundering governmental interference with the freedom of commerce, than the solemn parliamentary enactment of 1733 whose inefficacy, violation, and remoter consequences it was Mr. McClellan's special task to set forth.

Bryan Edwards wrote in 1793, in words as applicable to the trade of the foreign, as of the British, West Indies, "It may, I think, be affirmed, without hazard of contradiction, that if ever there was any one particular branch of commerce in the world, that called less for restraint and limitation than any other, it was the trade which, previous to the year 1774, was carried on between the planters of the West Indies and the inhabitants of North America." [1]

The philosophy of *laisser faire* is unquestionably inadequate to certain exigencies of our time, but the past achievements of state

Dublin Edition, II., p. 377.

regulation of trade might well bespeak a little more caution and modesty in the facile reasonings of some cavalier *étatisme* of the present day.

What field more alluring to state intervention than where humanity cries for social insurance? Yet it is a German professor who even here raises the question "si nous n'obtenons pas le contraire de ce que nous avons ambitionné, si nous n'asservissons pas des forces psychiques, alors que nous avons voulu les libérer, si nous ne créons pas la dépendance là où nous avons désiré l'indépendance."[1]

If the Molasses Act might conceivably have contemplated any imperial object, it sought to support the British power; in the outcome it contributed largely to the loss of the American empire.

And that the irony of events might nowise fail, the colonial patriots who championed in New England the principles of English liberty received something of their initial impulse to the contest for freedom and free molasses from the threatened curtailment of their profits in the distillation of intoxication for African

[1] Journ. des Économistes, juillet, 1912, p. 26.

tyrants and the thriving business of negro en-
slavement, a trade apparently still plied from
the city of the Puritans in the years when South
Carolina, like Virginia, was being opposed by
the British Government in her effort to restrict that travesty of commerce, while the
self-willed little colony that was the greatest
smuggler and slaver of them all was a leader
among the others not simply in her religious
and political freedom, but even in early, though
forgotten, anti-slavery legislation.

The noble agitations of the revolutionary
epoch, availing much for the black man as for
the white, failed, alas! to do enough, and it
may be some minor portion of that national
retribution of which George Mason warned his
countrymen, that the fair vision of commercial
freedom, which, but for New England's "com-
promise of iniquity," might seem to have
shone before the Republic at its birth, should
in the later days have become so clouded and
obscured, to the entailing of political evil, in
very consequence of the struggles engendered
by the Nation's congenital curse.

It appears to be the case that, in the gener-
ation before the Revolution at least, consider-

ably greater effort was made to enforce the law
under the royal governors of Massachusetts
Bay than in the charter colony of Rhode Island,
a discrimination resented by the merchants of
Boston which apparently contributed not a
little to the revolutionary spirit and promi-
nence of that port. It would be indeed interesting to speculate whether events might have
been appreciably altered had there been uniform enforcement or uniform laxity in all the
colonies. Modern difficulties springing from
variations of law or its enforcement in different
and competing jurisdictions had thus this interesting prototype.

But the study of colonial smuggling must
at least raise a deeper, and perhaps a sadder,
question, the question whether sensitive regard
for the majesty of law still suffers amongst the
American people from the injury wrought by
the foolish legislative officiousness of an eigh-
teenth-century English Parliament.

An effort has been made to free this essay
from any material error of statement or quota-
tion, but both the author and the undersigned
wil be grateful for information of any in-
accuracies that may be found.

If any reader of Mr. McClellan's essay shall be led as was the undersigned, to seek wider acquaintance with the contemporary pamphleteers or administrators cited in its pages, the essayist will have done his best service, and his reader be amply repaid for entry into a field rich in interest, replete with the fascination of a past close-linked, yet contrasting, with the present, the strongly-individualized elder brother of To-day.

DAVID TAGGART CLARK,

Assistant Professor of Economics.

WILLIAMS COLLEGE, October, 1912.

SMUGGLING IN THE AMERICAN COLONIES

CHAPTER I

COLONIAL TRADE

WITH the discovery of America in 1492, and the rounding of Africa by Da Gama in 1497,[1] supplemented by the discovery of the Pacific in 1513 and by Magellan's voyage six years later, commerce left its narrower bounds and became world-wide. The ports on the shores of the Mediterranean yielded commercial supremacy to those on the shores of the Atlantic. England, France, Denmark, Portugal, and Holland followed in the wake of Spain to America, attracted by the prospects of great wealth. To commercial enterprise can be attributed the discovery and rapid development of the West Indies and the North American continent. Much of

Expansion of Commerce

[1] For an account of the Spanish explorations, see E. G. Bourne *Spain in America*, chaps. III-X.

the work of exploration and colonization was left in the hands of trading companies and individuals who incurred the necessary risks for the sake of the expected returns.

The natural route for the early traders to follow was that of which Columbus was the pioneer. The West Indies, therefore, became the earliest great trading centre of the **Reasons for** New World commerce. Sugar, tobacco, cot-**Growth of Trade** ton, coffee, and other products of the Islands, **Between** were in great demand in Europe, for hereto-**England and the** fore the supply of most of these commodities **West Indies** had been exceedingly limited, and their cost had caused them to be classed almost as luxuries. Spain and Portugal had always considered that the foreign trade which brought into the realm the largest quantities of gold and silver was the most profitable.[1] The traders of those countries, therefore, early gave much of their attention to the South American continent where the mines needed only development to yield almost unlimited quantities of the precious metals.

[1] Cf. E. G. Bourne, *Spain in America*, page 142. "To the South, to the South, for the riches of the Aequinoctiall they that seek riches must go, not unto the cold and frozen North."—Peter Martyr, *De Rebus Oceanicis*, dec. VIII., lib. X, in Hakluyt, *Voyages*, V. 475.

Not only was the importation of gold and silver counted by these countries as the chief function of foreign trade, but prohibition was placed on their exportation. Thus the traders of these countries were deprived of the legitimate use of the instrument of commerce, economically considered the most useful. In England and France, from the seventeenth century on, the exportation of coin alone was prohibited while even that restriction was lacking in Holland. These three nations, abandoning Bullionism for Mercantilism, moved forward towards the principle made famous by Adam Smith that "The importation of gold and silver is not the principal, much less the sole, benefit which a nation derives from its foreign trade. Between whatsoever places foreign trade is carried on, they all of them derive two distinct benefits from it. It carries out that surplus part of the product of their land and labour for which there is no demand among them and brings back in return for it something else for which there is a demand."[1] Holland advanced farthest toward this principle, though even she fell far short of

[1] Adam Smith, *The Wealth of Nations*, bk. IV, chap. I.

its full acceptance. Considering the English trade alone, it is evident that by reason of the nature of the products of the West Indies, and by reason of the requirements of the two sections, the inevitable result would be the upbuilding of a great trade. The demand for the products of the Islands came to be hardly less constant than the demand for money itself, and each country produced principally that which the other could not produce and sorely needed.

West Indies Trade with North America

The reasons which led to the rapid growth of commerce between England and the West Indies held equally in regard to the development of trade which the establishment of the North American colonies opened up.[1]

[1] Lord Sheffield's figures for the trade between England and the West Indies are

	Imports from West Indies	Exports to
Av. 1700—1710	£629,127	£313,038
Av. 1760—1770	273,334	1,133,233

"Observations," App., table No. 9, page 20.

The decrease in imports into Great Britain is an apparent decrease rather than a real one. As we shall later see, the Islands sent the greater part of their products, rum and molasses, to the Northern colonies, receiving therefrom products which Great Britain could not so readily supply. Much of their products was subsequently re-exported to England from the American colonies.

The West Indies were placed between two markets whose demands always exceeded the supply and from each of which they could draw in return those goods, manufactured or natural, without which they would be seriously handicapped.

The history of the slave trade in the West Indies begins almost simultaneously with the discovery of the Islands, although the first strong impetus to the traffic was received when Spain authorized an importation of four thousand slaves into the Spanish islands.[1] An idea of the extent of this traffic can be gained best from the figures furnished by Bryan Edwards, the historian of the West Indies, who states that from 1700 to 1786 not less than 610,000 slaves were imported into Jamaica alone.[2] Aside from its extent, the slave trade was of importance economically because

The Slave Trade in the West Indies

[1] The Spanish government in 1517, arranged for the importation of four thousand slaves in eight years. Continuously after that time contracts were made with slave dealers to import slaves in increasing numbers. The business between 1609 and 1615 was conducted in the king's name. Cf. E. G. Bourne, *Spain in America,* American Nation Series, III, chap. XVIII.

[2] Edwards estimates that from 1680 to 1786, 2,130,000 slaves were imported into all the British colonies in America. *Hist. of W. I.,* Bk. IV, Ch. II.

it was only through it that the sugar cultivation was fostered.

The West Indies offered strong attractions to the traders of European nations. The vessel laden with a miscellaneous cargo of manufactured goods could find many ports which offered numerous customers. It must always be remembered, however, that this trade was fraught with unusual dangers. The presence of pirates and near-pirates had to be reckoned with. The formation of the Islands rendered them particularly suitable for the *rendezvous* of all kinds of freebooters. Constant warfare between European nations greatly stimulated privateering and their contests over the possession of one or another of the islands added to the dangers of commerce and made any restrictive law, which any one nation might enact, little better than a dead letter.

Character of Early Traders

It is doubtful if many of the traders themselves were of a much better class than the pirates. Admiral Penn has been described, though perhaps with some exaggeration, as "little better than the piratical sea-dog of his time."[1] The navigators of the age, if not

[1] Fiske, *The West Indies*, 79.

law-disregarding by nature, were bold and daring by necessity. Consequently if the ready customers were not forthcoming, the trader could often force an exchange on some of the weaker islanders or find a readier market at some unrestricted port. These possibilities of breaking through the commercial restrictions universal in the age aided materially in establishing the commercial position of the West Indies.

The effect which this type of traders and their methods had on the rapidly disappearing native islanders and the colonists, not of the highest character at best, could hardly have been other than to create an eager and tacit acceptance of smuggling and all kinds of illicit trade as matters of course. Such was the heritage which they bequeathed to the island inhabitants of the succeeding centuries and it was with much the same spirit, accentuated by a keener commercial capacity, that their descendants entered into trade relations in that later period when the trade between the West Indies and the North American continent became, as we shall see, essential to the development of the latter.

The Effect of Early Trade Conditions

CHAPTER II

ENGLISH COMMERCIAL SYSTEM

WHEN Grenville became the practical head of George III's government in 1763, a more thorough attempt was made than ever before to enforce the Acts of Trade and Navigation. Fully to understand the scope of these acts it is necessary to go back more than a century. Almost all additions after that of the 7th and 8th of William III merely added points of detail or aimed to facilitate the execution of the laws of this class passed in the seventeenth century. A careful study of these acts reveals Sponsors of England's Commercial System the fact that behind them stood as sponsors and chief beneficiaries the merchants and shipping interests. It was they who reaped the lion's share of the benefits and not, except as shipping favored naval defense, the British people. In the Ordinance of 1645 it is stated that "Nothing more enricheth this Kingdome than commerce." This proposition was the basis on which the early acts rested. Theoretically, increased commerce was to result in greater wealth in Great Britain, especially for the people as a whole; practically, the wealth was absorbed by the great merchants and ship-owners, and the people received such benefits as they did only very indirectly. Those indirect advantages accruing to them from the colonial system, as distinct from the Navigation Laws, were more than offset by the expense of the system and the cost of the whole colonial scheme of the period. After the Stuarts until 1763 revenue for the public treasury was only a minor part of the commercial program. Bancroft, quoting from the Grenville Papers, says that an American revenue of less than £2000 cost Great Britain £7000 or £8000 a year to collect.[1]

England could point to precedent in adopting the maritime policy about to be described, inasmuch as every other sea-power of Europe had and was enforcing a similar plan, attended often with much more severity. The Spanish colonies could trade legally with Spain alone and until 1765 and later their trade had to

Precedent for Commercial Policy of England

[1] III, 31. See also Fisher, *The Struggle for American Independence*, 51.

go almost wholly to one port, first Seville, then Cadiz.[1] Portugal formulated similar restrictions for the Brazilian trade, while France and Holland confined their colonies only less closely. It was therefore the system which seemed the natural one and every act of trade formed a step in the upbuilding of the whole structure.

Lord Sheffield in his "Observations on American Commerce," writing when our colonial period had just closed, remarks, "The only use and advantage of American Colonies or West Indies Islands is in the monopoly of their consumption and the carriage of their produce." His sweeping statement represents the extreme view of the protectionists but nevertheless contains one guiding motive of the commercial legislation. The monopoly feature was considered essential by all. G. L. Beer, referring to the earlier period, gives as the standard by which England measured the value of her colonies, the ability of the colony to produce "commodities that the mother country would otherwise have to buy from foreigners."[2] Properly and legally to secure to

Monopoly Feature

---

[1] See E. G. Bourne, *Spain in America*, chap. xix.
[2] G. L. Beer, *British Colonial Policy*, 135.

the mother country this advantage it was enacted in 1660: "That from and after the First Day of April, 1661, no Sugars, Tobacco, Cotton-Wool, Indicoes, Ginger, Fustick or other dying Wood, of the Growth, Production, or Manufacture of any English Plantations in America, Asia, or Africa shall be shipped, carried, conveyed, or transported from any of the English Plantations in America to any Land, Island, Territory, Dominion, Port, or Place whatsoever, other than to such other English Plantations as do belong to His Majesty, His Heirs and Successors, or to the Kingdom of England or Ireland, or Principality of Wales, or Town of Berwick upon Tweed, there to be laid on Shore, under Penalty of the Forfeiture of the said Goods, or the full Value thereof, as also of the Ship, with all her Guns, Tackle, etc."[1] In addition to these penalties, liability to forfeiture of bonds, required to bring the goods into lawful territory, was intended to make doubly sure the compliance with the law.

Direct Exportation Limited

The commodities specifically mentioned in this act formed what were called the "enumerated articles." The purpose of the forma-

[1] First Navigation Act. 12, Charles II, c. 18, 1660.

tion of this class was to give to the British merchant a monopoly in the distribution of these goods and to the English manufacturer a rich supply of raw materials and a virtually non-competitive market.[1]   While the non-enumerated articles could be carried at first to any part of the world, it must be remembered that legally after 1663 the colonists would usually have to return in ballast, or sell their ships, or meet the expenses of unloading and reloading at some English port. In final analysis, the act diminished profitable exportation from the colonies to any but English ports and it is self-evident that the purpose of the act was to favor the home country and that there was only secondary thought of revenue involved.

Enumerated Articles

Following quickly was the Act of 1663, which prohibited the bringing into the colonies, except from English ports, of commodi-

---

[1] The restrictions in this "enumerated" list were not as severe as would appear at first glance.   "None of the staple articles of the trade of New England were ever enumerated during the century 1660–1760,—neither fish, nor vessels, nor timber (except masts and bowsprits after 1706), nor rum; and during the whole period before us they could be carried wherever a market might be found."   W. J. Ashley, *Surveys*, page 315.   Tobacco, the staple product of Virginia, was thus at first the only continental commodity of importance on the list, and this was given by law a more than adequate market in England.

ties "of the Growth, Production or Manufacture of Europe."[1]   The preamble to this section furnishes an excellent illustration of the attitude assumed towards colonial possessions by England. It reads,—"And in regard His Majesty's Plantations beyond the Seas are inhabited and peopled by His Subjects of this, His Kingdom of England, For the maintaining a greater Correspondence and Kindness between them and keeping them in a firmer Dependence upon it, and rendring them yet more beneficial and advantageous unto it, in the farther Imployment and Encrease of English Shipping and Seamen, Vent of English Woolen and other Manufactures and Commodities, rendring the Navigation to and from the same more safe and cheap, and making this Kingdom a Staple, not only of the Commodities of those Plantations, but also of the Commodities of other Countries and Places, for the supplying of them, and it being the Usage of other Nations to keep their Plantation Trade to

Direct Importation Limited

Illustration of Britain's Attitude Towards Colonial Possessions

---

[1] 15, Charles II, c. 7, sec. VI.   Sec. VII of the same act makes exceptions in the case of salt for the New England and Newfoundland fisheries, of wines from Madeira and the Azores, servants and horses from Scotland and Ireland, etc.   In all cases, however, the shipping must be done in English vessels with English masters and crews.   The term "English" included colonial.

themselves, Be it enacted, . . . ''[1] While
the wording is made to indicate, in some places
that the colonists are to receive their share of
the expected boons, the preamble, as a whole,
leaves no doubt as to the intent of the law itself.

Other Provisions of Acts   The remaining provisions of the earlier
acts operated for the advantage of the co-
lonial almost as much as for the English
merchants.   Objections to them were of slight
importance and reflected local rather than
general conditions of commerce and sentiment.   Briefly, they were, (1) The confining
of the carrying trade to English or colonial
ships, whose master and three-fourths of
whose crews must be English;[2] (2) The
exclusion of foreigners from the coasting
trade;[3] (3) The prohibiting of aliens to
act as factors or merchants in the colonies.

Additions and Modifications   Subsequent acts added to the list of enumerated articles and more narrowly restricted
the number of ports to which non-enumerated
articles might be sent.   From time to time,
amendments were made designed to offset
some of the conditions which the colonists

[1] Second Navigation Act. 15, Charles II, c. 7, sec. V, 1663.
[2] 12, Charles II, c. 18. Sec. i., iii.
[3] 12, Charles II, c. 18, Sec. vi.

found most objectionable and about which they made the greatest complaint.

England, by these acts, was to play the part of producer or consumer or middleman in nearly every transaction in which the colonies figured. If the Continental nations were to trade directly with America, English merchants would be subjected to a competition unfair in the business conception of the time. For the colonies England was to be the great distributing point from which everything was to be received and to which many of the most important colonial products—all those, in fact, distinctively non-European in character—were exclusively to be sent. From the standpoint of the British merchant, the enforcement of these acts would create an ideal market in America, one in which he could sell high and buy low. From the standpoint of the British statesman, their enforcement would mean the realization of the ideal towards which European nations strove,—"A self-sufficient economic empire."[1]

Proposed Ideal Commercial Position of England

The great growth of trade between England and America is attested by these figures:

[1] G. L. Beer, *Col. Pol.*, 209.

Growth
of Trade
Between
England and
America

Encourage-
ments
Offered
American
Trade

the exports from the colonies increased from
£265,783 in 1710 to £1,044,591 in 1770,
while the imports rose from £267,205 to
£1,763,409 in the same years.[1]

If the upbuilding of a great trade between
England and America meant success to the
British trader, that very success carried with
it, in a smaller measure, the success of the
American trader. Each ship that came to
the colonies laden with the profit-bearing
goods of the Englishman departed laden with
goods whose sale meant profit, not always in
smaller degree, for the colonist. In fact, it is
not too much to say that much aid toward
promoting the prosperity of the colonies was
offered by the English authorities, with the
very important proviso, however, that in the
achieving of this prosperity, the interests of
the English merchants should always be

Twofold
Design of
Mercantile
Policy

maintained as paramount. In 1750 an act
was passed "to encourage the Importation
of Pig and Bar Iron from His Majesty's
Colonies in America; and to prevent the
Erection of any Mill or other Engine for

---

[1] Lord Sheffield, *Observations*, App., table No. 9, page 24.   Figures
are averages for the decades preceding each date.

Slitting or Rolling of Iron; or any Plateing Forge to work with a Tilt Hammer; or any Furnace for making Steel in any of the said Colonies."[1] This illustrates excellently the twofold design of the colonial policy. By admitting free of duty the pig-iron which could not be advantageously produced in England, encouragement is given to colonial activity in that pursuit, but this activity must cease when it reaches a point where the further development of the industry can be carried on with *Bounties* great profit in England. Earlier than this, during Anne's reign, bounties began to be paid for the importation into England, from America, of tar, pitch, rosin, turpentine, masts, yards, and bowsprits. Bancroft points out, however, that this relieved England of the necessity of depending upon Sweden for these essentials of the ship-builders' craft and of the navy.[2]

Pitkin, writing about 1817, mentions a society instituted in London some sixty years earlier "for the encouragement of arts, manufactures, and commerce," offering premiums

[1] 23, George II, ch. XXIX.
[2] G. Bancroft, *History of the United States*, II, 84.

for the production in the colonies and exportation to England of certain articles, mostly in
Premiums the raw state.[1] Virginia and Maryland tobacco planters were favored in laws, later repealed, which prohibited tobacco culture in England, a prohibition which for many years provoked great opposition although the unsuitableness of English soil and climate for raising tobacco of the finest quality early appeared.

The laws forbidding direct importation from the European Continent were made less severe by a system of rebates on the English duties. In most cases the duties that were paid on bringing merchandise into England for subsequent exportation to America were refunded excepting one-half of the so-called "old sub
Drawbacks sidy" of 5%. Therefore the charges were usu
and
Rebates ally less than the import duties for which the English consumer was held responsible. Furthermore, many of the articles which were among America's chief products, such as lumber, fish, salted provisions, and rum, were, as stated, not on the enumerated list and could,

[1] T. Pitkin, *Statistical View of the Commerce of the United States*, 12.

until 1766, be shipped to any part of the world, provided that the shipping was carried on in English or colonial bottoms, whose crews were three-fourths English and under an English master, although in 1764 hides and skins were put into the enumeration, and iron and lumber for a short time.

While an underlying motive, tending always to the giving of an advantage to the English manufacturer, merchant, or trader, can be found for the encouragements offered the colonists, it must in fairness be said, that it was not an entirely arbitrary method that England adopted to secure the monopoly of her colonial trade in America, but, rather, one constructed to give the appearances of partially mutual benefits, which were in a measure realized.[1]

Partially Mutual Benefits

In the new land of America the tilling of the soil yielded the richest returns, but it was natural that a number of the inhabitants turned their attentions and energies to other pursuits. Various manufactures, the knowledge of which had been brought from England, and other European countries, sprang

[1] See particularly Ashley, *Surveys*, 317–360.

up. The linen- and woolen-cloth makers, the paper-makers, the hat-makers, and the iron-makers began to ply their trades. Of course their products could not begin to supply all the demand of the rapidly growing colonies, but the effect of the increased supply was felt by the manufacturers in England and in 1731 the Board of Trade and Plantations was instructed to make a report "with respect to the laws made, manufactures set up, or trade carried on in the colonies detrimental to the trade, navigation, or manufactures of Great Britain." The findings of the Board were that the colonies north of Virginia, having less outlet for their natural products, were more likely to develop manufactures than those in the South. The difference in this regard had been observed by Sir Josiah Child, writing about 1668, "All our Plantations, except that of New-England, produce Commodities of different Natures from those of this Kingdom, as Sugar, Tobacco, Cocoa, Wool, Ginger, etc., whereas New-England produces generally the same we have here, viz., Corn and Cattle."[1]   In the possibility,

Colonial Manufactures

---

[1] *New Discourse of Trade*, 2nd ed., p. 213.

then, of the northern colonies' developing manufactures was a weakness in the protective wall being built around the English producer.

Jealousy on the part of the British manufacturer lay at the bottom of the acts formulated to restrict colonial manufacture. In addition to the danger of the curtailing of the colonial market, fears were entertained that the new rivals would begin exporting to European markets which the English were then supplying. As a matter of fact, the products of American manufacturing, with the possible exception of that of hat-making, supplied but a small part of the domestic needs. In Table two of Pitkin's "Statistical View" an account [1] of the articles exported from all the British continental colonies in the year 1770, when, if ever, the American manufactures would have been developed, shows scarce half a dozen items out of a possible sixty-four that could rightfully be classed as manufactured goods. Although some of the laws restricting manufacturing had been in force long before 1770, their effect on the volume of production was slight and

Manufacturing Interests Unimportant

[1] T. Pitkin, *Statistical View*, 2nd ed., 1817, pp. 21 ff.

the existence of the laws would not affect the value of the above citation.

The fear of competition, however, was so strong that, as early as the time of William III, when the woolen manufacture was prohibited to Ireland, pressure enough was brought to bear to allow the passage of an act, drastically worded in sum as follows, "After the First Day of December, 1669, no Wool or Manufactures made or mixt with Wool, being of the Product or Manufacture of any of the English Plantations in America, shall be loaden in any Ship or Vessel, upon any Pretence whatsoever—nor loaden upon any Horse, Cart, or other Carriage—to be carried out of the English Plantations to any other of the said Plantations, or to any other Place whatsoever."[1] One of the rather vague r asons advanced at the time for the necessity of this act was that colonial industry along the lines most profitable in England, would "inevitably sink the value of lands" in England, as the preamble has it. The interests of the landed gentry and of the wealthy classes were being carefully guarded. No trace of reciprocal

Manufactures Restricted

[1] 10 and 11, William III, ch. x.

benefits can be found in these enactments restricting manufactures. Nothing in them can be construed as aiding anyone but the British manufacturer or wool-grower.

We must not overlook the fact that while the inherent value of the colonies themselves was the main reason for which England for- mulated these laws, the commercial struggle with France, Spain, and especially Holland, in which England was then desperately en- gaged, allowed the spirit of business rivalry to have an undue influence. S. G. Fisher, seemingly without complete accuracy of detail, remarks on this point, "The first important product from the colonies was tobacco from Virginia; and the king, who could at that time,[1] without the aid of Parliament, impose duties and taxes, put a heavy duty on this tobacco from Virginia. The Virginians accordingly sent all their tobacco to Holland. This sim- ple instance shows both the cause and prin- ciple of all the navigation laws. If Holland, England's rival in commerce, was to reap all

---

[1] S. A. Morgan in the *History of Parliamentary Taxation*, pages 241 ff., discusses fully the question of the right of the king to collect imposts.

the advantage of Virginia's existence, of what value to England was Virginia?"[1] In part then for commercial jealousy the Virginians were ordered to ship only to England, where they were granted for a time a monopoly.[2]

Interesting it is to note the impression which this mercantile system made on the minds of the publicists of the time. Adam Smith, apostle of the new doctrine of free trade, admitted that England was less illiberal than other nations in administering the regulations, common to all nations of the age, but adds, "It can not be very difficult to determine who have been the contrivers of this whole commercial system; not the consumer, we may believe, whose interest has been entirely neglected, but the producers whose interest has been so carefully attended to; and among the latter class our merchants and manufacturers have been by far the principal architects."[3] Montesquieu, writing earlier, in 1748, was in favor of the system,

Contemporary Views of England's Commercial System

---

[1] S. G. Fisher, *The Struggle for American Independence*, I, 37.

[2] See G. L. Beer, *Commercial Policy*, pages 24–27, for discussion of the tobacco monopoly and the colonial trade with Holland; and *Origin of the British Colonial System*, pp. 108 ff.

[3] Adam Smith, *Wealth of Nations*, bk. IV, chap. viii, 3d edition.

because "the design of the settlement was the extension of commerce and not the founding of a city or a new empire" and considered that any loss to a colony, was "visibly compensated by the protection of the mother country who defends it by her arms and supports it by her laws."[1] The view of Adam Smith is less influenced by political considerations and the evident but unexpressed conclusion is that the whole system was based on economic principles that would not make for satisfactory relations between two peoples such as the English and their American colonists. Montesquieu, while grasping the motives which led to the colonization of America and the inception of the colonial policy, failed to recognize the nature and character of the people in America and the spirit which they had developed. His compensations for restraint may have been sound theoretically but, practically, were never pressed independently upon the minds of the colonists to the point where they might be deemed material compensations from their point of view. The colonists at the time did not consider as "com-

[1] Montesquieu, *The Spirit of the Laws*, bk. XXI, chap. xxi.

pensations" the part which England played in
the colonial defense or the protection to shore
and shipping which the British navy rendered.
Rather, they looked upon the privileges, permitted by the paternal system, as rights, which
they should enjoy without paying an extra
price for them.[1] In America, there were those
who believed that the best interests of the
colonies were being subserved by the operation
of the existing system.[2]

Such a system, developed through a century or more, by acts of kings and parlia-
ments, was the one which the colonies were
expected to accept. It was long in the evo-
lution, but such effect as it had on the period
immediately preceding the Revolution was as
though it had been created as a whole at that
time.

[1] Cf. G. E. Howard, *Preliminaries of the Revolution*, 63–67.

[2] See Fisher, *Struggle for American Independence*, 45. Also James
Otis, *The Rights of the British Colonies Asserted and Proved*, p. 58.
Cf. p. 76 (*Memorial*). "The validity of the general doctrine that the
mother country and not foreigners should supply the colonies, 'provided the Mother Country can and does supply her Plantations with
as much as they want,' was admitted in 1762 by the Virginia Com-
mittee of Correspondence in a letter to the colony's agent in London."
Beer, *Col. Pol.*, 207.

CHAPTER III

THE CAUSES AND CHARACTER OF COLONIAL SMUGGLING

ALL "illicit trade" and "smuggling" cannot be grouped in one class. Wherever laws are laid down there are those who evade them if possible and advantage is to be gained. This is especially true in the case of laws requiring the payment of duties. But unless restrictive commercial measures are opposed to some natural and essential channel of commerce, the evasion of them is of little significance except in so far as it illustrates the weakness of administrative officers and the greed of the law-breakers for gain acquired by any means, foul or fair.

When has "Illicit Trade" significance?

In general, the evasions of those of the Acts of Trade and Navigation which aimed to restrict the colonial trade to England, can probably not be considered as of prime importance. This statement is based principally on a study of Sheffield's "Observations on the

Slight Importance of Evasions of Acts Restricting Colonial Trade to England

Commerce of the American States." Lord
Sheffield was so situated that he had access to
trustworthy sources of information. Although
he set out to prove that the trade of America
would naturally go to England, the soundness
of his reasons and reasonings has been proven
by subsequent developments.[1]

Let us follow Sheffield's arguments more
closely. He sets forth a list of commodities,[2]
such as shoes, stockings, hats, porcelain,
woolens, iron and steel manufactures, glass,
earthenware, painters' colors, and other minor
articles, comprising nearly all the staple manufactures demanded by the American market.
Taking up each item separately, he shows
clearly that there could be but little competi-

[1] After the close of the Revolution, Lord Sheffield published his
"Observations on the Commerce of the American States," in which
he advised against the admission of American shipping to the ports
of the British West Indies. In his introduction, he says, "The question between us amounts only to this—Whether the British West
Indies can be supplied with lumber and provisions at a moderate
price, and their rum find a market without the admission of foreign
shipping into our Colonies? and whether the British dominions can
maintain shipping sufficient for their trade and supplies? The question is not, at present, whether the British dominions can supply
the British West Indies; but whether all the world can supply them in
British shipping?" Intro., page xiii. Theory plays but a small part
in his argument. The facts and statistics he uses include the
period preceding the Revolution.

[2] Op. cit., 6th edition, 1784, pp. 7–36.

tion for the British dealers in these commodities in the American market. The figures of Macpherson, though referring to the ante-bellum period of restriction, may be cited in this connection. In 1769, the official total value of imports into the colonies was £2,623,-412, of which £1,064,975 were from Great Britain and £789,754 were from the West Indies. The value of the importations from Africa was about £150,000, consisting principally of slaves and therefore negligible in this discussion. There remained then only £76,000 from "the South of Europe."[1] Sheffield next takes up the group of merchandise in which "there may be competition."[2] These, such as cheap tea, paper, silks, and fine linens, he asserts usually come to America through England, and Macpherson gives corroborating testimony by his citing the fact that of the great quantity of linen imported into London in 1731, from Holland and Germany, "the greatest part is again exported to our plantations in America, and our factories in Africa, etc."[3]

Reasons are given below for the course

England the Natural Trading Place for Colonies

---

[1] D. Macpherson, *Annals of Commerce*, III, 571–572.
[2] Op. cit., pp. 36–54. .   [3] Op. cit., III, 182.

which trade in these goods took; first, however, we may notice some of the infractions of
the English monopoly which took place.

Traders from Dutch ports were the chief
offenders in the matter of illegal tea importation into the colonies. One of their methods
was to clear for some Dutch colony with an
American port named as a port-of-call. Their
official papers would then protect them in a
measure in their operations at the American
port. Another method was for British vessels
from Holland to enter but a part of their cargo
with the custom-house officers at some British
port, thus paying duty on a small part only
of their cargo, while they "landed their entire

**Dutch Tea
Smuggling**
cargoes in the colonies."[1]   The tea thus smuggled in was of a cheap variety that the English merchants seldom handled and they, as
a rule, felt themselves secure in the control
of the market for the better grade of teas.
Much has been made of the tea smuggling of
the colonies, but G. L. Beer comes to the conclusion that the tea consumption has been
much over-estimated and that, therefore, the
disparity in the amount of tea said to have

[1] Beer, *Col. Pol.*, pp. 243 f.

been consumed and the amount legally imported from Great Britain, lacks the significance usually attached to it.[1]

Some French manufactures were smuggled into the colonies from the French islands, in connection with the trade presently to be described, but it is doubtful whether their amount was great.

England's position in the mercantile world had become a dominant one and to her came the products of all parts of the world. American vessels seeking general cargoes would find them more easily in the ports of England than in the ports of any other nation. Furthermore, British merchants were more disposed to give long credit to American merchants than were other foreign business men. The principal reason, however, to cause the trade of the colonies in many of the above mentioned articles to go to England was the accepted fact that England could produce better quality at a lower price. *Advantages of English Ports*

Macpherson's figures, quoted above, establish the fact that, either in spite of, or because of, natural tendencies, the colonists

[1] G. L. Beer, *British Colonial Policy*, 245 f, note 2.

did get their legal imports chiefly from England. For this there could have been but two explanations: first, that they found it to their advantage from a business standpoint; or, second, they felt constrained to do so on account of the regulations of the Acts of Trade and Navigation. Lord Sheffield, as trustworthy as any contemporary observer, says, "The preference formerly given (to England) was not the effect of our restrictions; nothing was easier to the Americans than to evade them; and it is well known that from the first, * * they uniformly did evade them whenever they found it to their interest."[1] Moral scruples had no more weight with the colonists in connection with the general import trade than they had in connection with the West Indies trade and we shall see that smuggling existed in the latter whenever the colonists found it to their advantage. We may therefore eliminate, to a large degree, the trade regulations as a coercing force in the English trade with the colonies.

Many great staples which England produced had overcome French, German, and Dutch

Growth of Trade Between England and Colonies Due to Natural Causes

[1] Op. cit., 234.

competitors in their home markets and it is reasonable to assume that the Americans would find it to their advantage to buy from the same producers. Even during and after the Revolution the advantage of trading in England was so great that James Madison wrote in 1785, "Our Merchants are almost all connected with that country and that only." [1]

We must therefore reiterate our former statement that, in all probability, the evasion of those Acts of Trade and Navigation which purposed to confine so much of the colonial import trade to England, was of comparatively minor significance only in the development of the revolutionary spirit of the colonists. Of course, exceptional cases existed but they are traceable usually to special causes of slight general importance. Probably the total amount of merchandise smuggled in, in connection with the European trade, was but a small part of the total volume of business.

In our discussion of the development of England's commercial system, we have purposely failed to mention the Molasses Act, Molasses passed in 1733. As an efficient restrictive Act

James Madison, "Works," I, 156; *Writings*, Hunt's ed., II, 147.

measure, its influence was naught; as an incentive to illicit trade, its importance was greater than that of any other trade regulating act, and it is its evasion principally rather than its effect on legitimate commerce that we are now to consider. From the very nature of the commerce at which it struck, its observance would have been well-nigh impossible. Briefly, the Molasses Act laid prohibitive duties upon the importation from the foreign Sugar Islands into the American colonies of rum, molasses, and sugar.[1]

We have seen that the chief products of the New England colonies were lumber and fish, and of the Middle colonies, agricultural

Disadvantages of Exporting Staples to England

staples. These two sections, especially the former, were also great ship-building and ship-owning centers. Of their products, part went to England, but the market was restricted, for, during the reign of Charles II, statutes were passed in behalf of the British farmers, practically prohibiting the importation of grain and meat into England, and the

[1] "Molasses Act was to continue in force five years; but it was five times renewed and by the Sugar Act of 1764 was made perpetual." Macdonald, *Documentary Source Book of American History*, 1908.

demand there for fish and lumber was not great enough to equal the supply. There remained a vast unconsumed surplus in the hands of the colonists for which, again, in the British West Indies, there was not a sufficient demand.

Of the courses then open to the colonists, either was likely to involve legal difficulties. First, they could manufacture for themselves, —a procedure not only legally restricted[1] but economically unwise if not impossible. Second, they could export to a third market, which was both a natural and a ready market—the foreign West Indies islands—but from which a return cargo was by the Molasses Act sought to be interdicted. The second course was the one adopted and the reasons seem to justify the selection.

Alternative Courses Open

Selection Made

The colonies depended on England for their manufactured goods, but the value of the products exported in return always left the balance of trade in favor of England. Money was therefore essential and enough of it could not be obtained in the British West

[1] 10 and 11 William III, chap. X., 19; 5 George II, chap. XXII; 23 George II, chap. XXIX.

Indies. The foreign islands were eager for
the colonial products and had an abundance
of money which their direct trading with
Europe yielded. From them, and from the
trade from the south of Europe, presently to
be referred to, the colonists obtained the
needed specie. But still more from the Islands they obtained those products on which
obtaining their specie ultimately depended.
The rum, and the molasses which the Boston
and Rhode Island distilleries soon made into
rum, were re-exported to Africa and in return
were brought back great numbers of slaves.
The slave market, both of the Islands and of
the Southern American colonies, was never
over-supplied.   Slave labor was of the greatest
moment in the production of the South's
great staples.   Rum was practically the only
commodity that could have been exchanged
for the African slaves and it is in this consideration that the Southern colonies became dependent on the trade between the Northern colonies and the West Indies, British and foreign.

The money derived from the West Indies
trade did not long remain in America, for the
balance of trade between England and Amer-

Colonists
Could
Secure
Needed
Money
Only on the
Basis of the
West Indies
Trade

ica was, as stated above, always in favor of
England and to a very large degree. No division of opinion among contemporary or modern writers is discernible on this point.
Colden, in 1723, asserted that money coming
from the West Indies "seldom continues six
months in the Province, before it is remitted
for England."[1] He carried his later observations to the logical conclusion by declaring,
in 1764, "It is evident to a demonstration
that the more Trade the Colonies in North
America have with the Foreign Colonies, the
more they consume of the British Manufactures."[2] Franklin's explanation of the differ-

Final Destination of Money Derived from West Indies Trade

---

[1] *Documents relative to the Colonial History of New York*, V, 686.

[2] Ibid. VII, 612. In 1767, Dennis de Berdt, agent for Massa-
chussetts in London, presented a memorial to the Board of Trade,
in which he said, "To put any difficulties on the American Trade,
will inevitably diminish our exports to that Country, from their inability to pay the Merchants for the Manufactures imported by
them, which inability will be the same whether the people in America resolve to take goods or not." A. B. Hart, *History told by Contemporaries*, II, No. 146; quoting from "*Papers relating to Public
Events in Massachusetts preceding the Revolution* (1856)."

Compare argument of John Ashley, a Barbados planter, who, in a
pamphlet, "*Some Observations on a direct exportation of sugar from the
British Islands*, in a letter from a gentleman in Barbadoes to his friend
in London" (Dec. 21, 1734) writes, "The Planters will never want a
Supply of British Goods when they have the wherewithal to pay
for them; and the more Markets they have to take off their Products,
the better able will they be to pay for what they want, and the more
they will take off; and such Supplies will come from Great-Britain,

ence in the value of the English commodities imported into Pennsylvania, £500,000, and the value of those articles exported directly to England, £40,000, was that the balance due England was made up by the trade with the English, French, Spanish, Dutch, and Danish West Indies; and this explanation may be considered as typical for the New England colonies as well.

On their side of the case, the French Islands were prohibited from sending rum to France for fear of interfering with the French brandy trade. As it was essential for the islanders to dispose of their greatest product, rum, and particularly molasses, became the chief articles offered on advantageous terms in exchange for the products of the North.

Of equal force was the economic necessity which compelled the continental colonies to export to the foreign West Indies. This arose principally from the nature of the commodities produced. Disregarding the influ-

some how or other, and in Time, either the Planters will send Effects to their Factors in Great-Britain for them, or they will buy them of the British Merchants' Factors in the Islands, as they find most for their Convenience and Advantage." op. cit., page 17.

ence of the legal hindrances to European trade noted above, we may assume that the supply of commodities would have sought the market where there was the greatest demand. The following statistics show conclusively that the demand of the West Indies was far in excess of that of England. New England sent to the Islands, in 1770, staves and headings and hoops for barrels and hogsheads to the value of about £70,000, or about three times as much as was sent to England. Bread and flour, principally from Pennsylvania, to the amount of 23,449 tons were exported to the Islands in comparison with 263 tons sent to England. West Indies Practically the Only Adequate Market Open to the Colonists

In the shipping of fish, we find that, of the better, dried fish, 431,386 quintals went to the south of Europe, legally permissible, 206,081 quintals to the West Indies, and only 22,086 to Great Britain. Of the products of the fisheries, however, there remained a great quantity of low grade pickled fish which could find an adequate market only in the West Indies, which consumed 29,582 barrels of a total 30,068.[1] In 1778, John Adams observed, Importance of Fisheries

[1] Pitkin, *Statistical View*, 2nd ed., 1817, table II, furnishes these figures.

"One part (the low grade) of our fish went to the West Indies for rum, and molasses to be distilled into rum, which injured our health and our morals; the other part (the high grade) went to Spain and Portugal for gold and silver, almost the whole of which went to London." [1] It is readily seen that the profit of the fisheries was dependent on a market for the whole catch, and that if the foreign West Indies market had been taken away, the success of the whole business would have been jeopardized. Minot states the possible result of this, succinctly, in the following, "The business of the fishery * * was at this time estimated at £164,000 per annum; the vessels employed in it, which would be nearly useless, at £100,000; the provisions used in it, the casks for packing fish, and other articles, at £22,700 and upwards; to all of which there was to be added the loss of the advantage of sending lumber, horses, provisions and other commodities to the foreign plantations as cargoes, * * and the dismissing of 5,000 seamen from their employment." [2]

Success of Fisheries Dependent on West Indies Trade

[1] Sparks, *Diplomatic Correspondence of the Revolution*, IV, 273.
[2] G. R. Minot, *History of Massachusetts*, II, 147, quoting from the arguments of Mauduit, the agent of Massachusetts in England.

Except for the indirect advantage in connection with the supply of slaves, noted above, and which should not be underemphasized, the dependence of the Carolinas, Virginia, and the other Southern colonies upon the West Indies trade was not of importance. Their great natural products, rice and tobacco, except during short intervals, were afforded by law markets that were extensive enough to demand all their surplus production, and from these markets they could draw back money or manufactured goods in exchange. The balance of trade being more nearly equal, their demand for gold and silver could be supplied without recourse to the West Indies. To interfere, however, with the trade that was being carried on between the foreign West Indies islands and the northern American colonies would have been an interruption fraught with the gravest results. From the very nature of the commodities most prominent in the trade and from the geographical position of the two sections, the one party in the transactions supplied the only possible adequate market for the products of the other party, while, in the situation, the mate-

Situation in Southern Colonies Different

Molasses Act Remains Unenforced

rial life and growth of each was largely dependent on what it received from the other.[1]   Had the markets of Europe been wholly unrestricted, the larger ships required and the difficulty of the voyage would have served as hindrances to trade, while these hindrances were almost entirely lacking in trade between the Islands and America. As the Molasses Act remained unenforced, this natural trade was allowed to develope to the fullest, and each year's non-enforcement was making more difficult the situation which the British customs-officials had to face, finally, in 1763. It is a question whether the term "smuggling" is a proper one to apply to the evasions of the Molasses Act that occurred previous to that time, inasmuch as, with the exception of a

[1] A concise statement of the interdependence of the North American and West Indies trade is given as follows by Governor Pownall; "The West India islands produce sugar, molasses, cotton, etc.; they want the materials for building and mechanics, and many the necessaries of food and raiment: The lumber, hides, the fish, flour, provisions, live-stock, and horses, produced in the northern colonies on the continent, must supply the islands with these requisites.   On the other hand, the sugar and molasses of the sugar islands is become a necessary intermediate branch of the North American trade and fisheries.   The produce of the British sugar islands cannot supply both Great Britain and North America with the necessary quantity; this makes the molasses of the foreign sugar islands also necessary to the present state of the North American trade."   Thomas Pownall, *Administration of the Colonies*, 4th Edition, 1768, London, pp. 5 f.

brief period of activity about 1760 custom-houses ignored or winked at the importations from the West Indies. This long non-enforcement of the act directed against the natural trade of the colonies, enables Mellen Chamberlain to present the position of the colonists when the enforcement of the Sugar Act was imminent, in these words, "The other party (the colonists), basing their claim on natural equity and long enjoyment, wished to retain it (the West Indies trade)." [1]

The duties [2] which the Molasses Act sought to levy on imports to the colonies from the foreign West Indies were such as to have the effect of an absolute prohibition of trade between them. They were intended to be regulative and not revenue-producing. The sole *raison d'être* of the act was to protect the interests of the British West Indies. The fact that they operated to the disadvantage of the British colonies in North America to an infinitely greater degree did not alter the determination of the framers of the act, al-

Interests of British West Indies Considered of Greater Importance than those of American Colonies

---

[1] J. Winsor, *Narrative and Critical History of America*, VI, 23–24.

[2] The duties which the Molasses Act sought to levy were,—On rum and spirits, 9d. per gallon; on molasses and syrups, 6d. per gallon; on sugars, 5s. per cwt.

though it is open to conjecture whether the recognition of this fact did not furnish partial grounds for the non-enforcement of the act. Perhaps, too, a tardy realization of the fact that its enforcement would lead to a lessening of the ability of the Americans to purchase from English merchants was of some weight in the non-enforcement. England always considered the interest of the British islands as of greater importance than that of her North American possessions. The Islands were **Reasons for Favors Shown British Islands** deemed economically much more useful to the mother country by reason of the nature of their resources. The great plantations were owned by English gentlemen most of whom resided in England and who were in close touch with the government and thus more likely to have their complaints listened to. We may again quote Beer, who gives as the standard by which England measured the value of her colonies, the ability of the colony to "produce commodities that the mother country would otherwise have to buy from foreigners." "Hence greater stress was laid on colonies as sources of supply than as markets for British manufacturers." Judged by this

standard, the West Indies, except for naval Standards for Judging Colonial Values
supplies, would rank as much more important
than the continental, especially the Northern,
colonies. Bancroft describes the commercial
activity of the West Indies as that of "bees
carrying all their honey to England." This
method of comparing colonial values was in
vogue at the time of the passage of the Molasses Act and continued until about 1763, when
England began to esteem her manufacturing
interests more highly and to consider the
colony affording the best market as the one
deserving of the greater consideration. Of
this somewhat altered view the dictum of
Sheffield, above cited, is evidence.

Nowhere was there a keener realization of
the favored position of the West Indies than
in the Islands themselves, and among those
financially interested in them. This sense
of security in governmental favor reached
such a point that the attempt was actually
made first to prohibit in terms most of the Efforts of the British West Indies to Confine Trade to Themselves
trade of the North American colonies with the
foreign islands. A bill towards this end
passed the House of Commons but memo-
rials to the House of Lords by the colonial

assemblies prevented its final passage.[1]   The
question of why the Molasses Act remained
unenforced is one principally of conjecture
unless we seek the explanation in the weak
organization of the customs service.   Since
1696, the Board of Trade and Plantations was
in general charge of colonial affairs.   It was a
sub-committee of the Privy Council.   The
Board received most of its information from
the governors of the provinces, who were between two fires in the matter of giving information concerning evasions of law.   The
governors and the two Surveyors-General of
Organiza-   Customs,[2] North and South, were assisted in the
tion of
Customs   administration of the laws by the "naval
Service   officers" and the collectors, with surveyors and
searchers at each principal port. The personnel
of the service at best was one hardly com-
manding much respect. The collectorships were
sometimes delegated, the appointees remaining
in England and entrusting the actual work to
deputies.   While the collectors were never

[1] *Pennsylvania Archives.*   Series IV, Vol. I, pp. 482 f. and 493 ff.
[2] Good accounts of the organization of the customs service are
found in Scharf & Westcott's *History of Philadelphia*, III, 1800, ff., in
G. E. Howard, *Preliminaries of the Revolution*, 72, and in G. L. Beer,
British Commercial Policy, pages 123 ff.

popular, it is significant that acts of violence were uncommon before 1755 and reached their worst after 1763.

It was only with the connivance of the custom-house officials that much of the illegal trade was possible. The connivance is, however, greatly illuminated by the discretionary power conferred upon the collectors by a statute of Charles II,[1] to accept partial payment of the statutory duties as full payment. The methods, however, employed by the smugglers were legion, false clearance papers, partial entries, and mis-labeled packages being **Connivance** some of the ways by which illicit entry was **of Officials** made by the larger vessels. The bays and rivers afforded ample opportunities for the smaller vessels to run in their entire cargoes without detection. Governor Bernard of Massachusetts wrote in 1764, "If conniving at foreign sugars and molasses and Portugal wines and fruits is to be reckoned corruption, there never was, I believe, an uncorrupt custom officer in America until within twelve months." From the same source we have the following statement concerning the 15,000 hogsheads of

[1] 13 and 14 Ch. II, c. 11, §§ xvii, xviii.

molasses imported into Massachusetts in 1763, "all of which, except less than 500, came from Ports which are now Foreign."[1] It was estimated that the duty on molasses, if collected, would amount to £25,000 a year.[2] For the officials, however, it should be said that smuggling was a less heinous crime in those days than later. In England there existed a great system of illicit trade with which were believed

Attitude Toward Smuggling in England and America to be connected "gentlemen of rank and character in London."[3] In America, the long laxity in enforcement of the Molasses Act led to its being considered as a dead letter and with its evasions are connected such names as that of Fanueil[4] in Boston.

The violation of trade regulations in connection with the West Indies trade, that resulted in the most serious and momentous conse-

Contraband Trade with French quences arose at the time of the Seven Years' War between England and France. The American colonies and the French islands

---

[1] From Quincy's *Mass. Reports*, pp. 423 f., and Bernard's *Select Letters on the Trade and Government of America in the years 1763–1768*, p. 10.

[2] John Adams, *Works*, X, 348.

[3] Fisher, Op. cit., 51.

[4] W. B. Weeden, *Economic and Social History of New England*, II, 620; cf. pp. 612 and 627 f.

had become so interdependent that at the outbreak of hostilities between their mother
countries, the commercial intercourse between
them did not cease, notwithstanding the fact
that at the beginning of the war distinct
measures were passed by both the colonial
and the Home governments to break up the
trade.[1] Finally, in 1757, after having been
urged to put the colonial food-products into
"the enumeration," Parliament forbade, during the period of the war, the export of any
food supplies, except fish and rice, to any place
outside the British dominions. The French
were entirely dependent upon the northern
products for their chief food supplies. The
American colonies were called upon to supply
financial aid for England [2] which was waging
war principally in their behalf, and the colonies needed then, if ever, the West Indies trade
from which they drew their chief profit and
so much of their specie. Although the con-

[1] For the interesting acts of the colonial assemblies, see Beer, Colo‑
nial Policy, pp. 77 f.

[2] The preamble to the "Sugar Act" states that the revenues,
prescribed by it, are levied because "it is just and necessary, that a
Revenue be raised in" his American colonies "for defraying the
Expenses of defending, protecting, and securing the same."—4 George
III, chap. xv.

tinuance of the trade by the Americans may have indicated a break in the sympathy of the colonies with England, it is fair to conjecture that a desire for business profits and the economic necessity for the continuance of the trade, were the motives at bottom.   This trade with the enemy was carried on in two ways: either with the French directly under "Flags of Truce," or indirectly through the neutral islands of other nations.

Motives at the Bottom of Contraband Trade

The "Flags of Truce" were originally issued by the colonial governors for the purpose of allowing vessels to exchange prisoners with the French.   This system had already begun in the earlier wars of the century.   Many abuses of the system arose.   With the prisoners was carried merchandise which was also exchanged, and when the exchange of prisoners was effected, the permits were not surrendered but were used for subsequent expeditions. Pennsylvania was perhaps the worst offender in the abuse of this practice.   Governor Denny publicly sold these permits to the highest bidders and there was such a large number of ships engaged in this trade that James Hamilton, Lieutenant-Governor, on information of

" Flags of Truce "

Sir Jeffrey Amherst that provisions were being collected in Philadelphia to send to the French fleet and army in the West Indies, directed the Collector of Customs at Philadelphia to hold there all ships except those released by special warrant.[1] Rhode Island was second only to Pennsylvania in making possible the violations of the privileges of the "Flags of Truce." In Virginia, the Lieutenant-Governor was offered four hundred guineas if he "would license a Flag of Truce," but he refused the offer.[2]

The ease with which the indirect trade with the French was conducted was greatly enhanced by the practice of the European nations of allowing the commerce of certain ports in their West Indies possessions to be free to the whole world. Holland had as a "free port" the island of St. Eustatius, Denmark allowed to St. Thomas entire commercial freedom, while France and England possessed such ports in St. Domingo, and in Jamaica and Dominica. The evident purpose of such

Indirect Trade with the French

---

[1] *Pennsylvania Archives*, Series IV, Vol. III, 144. A general embargo was laid by Pennsylvania to break up the "Flag of Truce" trade, but it was of short duration.

[2] G. L. Beer, *British Colonial Policy*, 90.

a feature in an otherwise stringent system was to make possible the drawing away of trade from commercial rivals. The purpose was undoubtedly accomplished but, at the same time, smuggling was greatly abetted thereby, and the Dutch and Spanish became intermediaries in the illicit trade between the English and the French.

England's undoubted supremacy on the sea forced the French to throw open their ports to the Dutch, against whom they were usually closed. The British vice-admiralty courts in the West Indies then had a legal or semi-legal ground on which to justify the seizure of Dutch ships as carriers of contraband of war under the provisions of the "Rule of 1756." The strength of the British navy, backed by the authority of the courts, was sufficient to break up to a great extent the part which the Dutch were playing in the transportation of provisions from the American colonists to the French.

Another go-between was found in the Spanish settlement of Monte Christi. As a market or as a source of supply, this port could not of itself have been attractive to

American shipping interests, but the cause of the sudden growth of its commerce lay in the fact that it was contiguous to French territory. To make the conduct of business more easy, crown subjects from North America resided at the port and small French vessels were employed to transfer the provisions directly to French soil, so that the trade could almost be classed as a direct trade with the enemy. Its great extent is attested by the observations of the commanders of British war-vessels sent to investigate. At the time at which His Majesty's sloop, *Viper*, was at Monte Christi on Feb. 5, 1759, twenty-eight of the twenty-nine ships there were from the North American colonies. In May, 1761, a Captain Hinxman reported that, of fifty vessels in port, thirty-six were from North America.[1] Governor Haldane of Jamaica made affidavits on June 9, 1759 that at times from one hundred to one hundred and twenty North American vessels were at Monte Christi.[2] There could have been but one object back of

---

[1] G. L. Beer, *British Colonial Policy*, 98, note 2, quoting from the Board of Trade Papers and Home Office Papers.
[2] Ibid., 99, note 4.

the visits of all these vessels to this port at this particular time.

British Objections to Trade with French The objections raised by the British civil and military authorities, both before and after the Parliamentary Act of 1757, were natural and reasonable. The supplying of the enemy with provisions and the sinews of war, unobtainable elsewhere, was inherently treasonable, and by the Act of 1757, was also a form of smuggling. Further, the exportation of large quantities of staples, such as flour and bread, diminished the supply in America when the demand was abnormally large on account of the quartering of a great army of British and colonial troops. The attending rise in prices made it cheaper for the military commissary to import supplies from England, yet the elements of risk and delay in the long carriage rendered this undesirable, except when the necessity was urgent. G. L. Beer has ferreted out a seemingly inexhaustible mass of evidence from the official papers and correspondence in the English Public Record Office, all of which seems to show that the complaints of the officials were warranted by the facts.[1]

[1] G. L. Beer, *British Colonial Policy*, chapter vi and notes.

Their alarm was great enough to cause the establishment of a general embargo, whose life however was short.[1]

Pitt on Aug. 23, 1760, summed up the matter of illegal trade with the enemy in his instructions to Provincial Governors in these words: "The Commanders of His Majesty's Forces and Fleets, in North America and the West Indies, having transmitted repeated and certain Intelligence of an illegal and most pernicious Trade, carried on by The King's Subjects in North America, and the West Indies, as well to the French Islands, as to the French Settlements on the Continent of America . . . by which the Enemy is, to the greatest Reproach and Detriment of Government, supplied with Provisions, and other Necessaries, whereby They are principally, if not alone, enabled to sustain and protract this long and expensive War; . . . In order therefore to put the most speedy Stop to such Practices . . . so highly repugnant to the Honor and Wellbeing of this Kingdom, it is His Majesty's express Will that you do forthwith make the strictest Enquiry into the State of this dangerous and ignominious Trade."[2]

[1] Beer, *Col. Pol.*, 113; cf. 85.　[2] Gray, in *Quincy's Mass. Reports*, 407.

To attempt to explain the motives which prompted the colonies to engage in this treasonable form of illicit trade, by ascribing them to a developing spirit of independence, **Political Arguments Against Contraband Trade with French** would call up a series of counter-arguments worth considering. In the first place, the colonists were simultaneously and voluntarily aiding England with troops and money in her struggle with France in North America, although it is true that this aid was rendered often with reluctance. In the second place, the final triumph of France in America, toward which this contraband trade aided, would simply mean the transferring of the nominal authority over the colonies from England to France, whereas we have seen that the natural relations, both political and commercial, of the colonies were with England.[1] And, finally, it may be assumed that the colonists recognized that if the English succeeded in completely breaking the French power in America, there would be removed the need which the colonies

[1] Jeremiah Dummer, agent for Massachusetts in London from 1710 to 1721, "shows how early and passionate among the English colonies in America was the dread of the American power of France," declaring,"that those colonies can never be easy or happy, 'whilst the French are masters of Canada.'" G. E. Howard, *Preliminaries of the Revolution*, VIII, 6, quoting Tyler, *Am. Lit.*, II, 119.

had always felt for British protection. In view of these three considerations, it appears that every possible political argument would lead to the offering of every aid by the colonists to England. It must be the assumption, then, that economic reasons urged more strongly the continuance of the trade than political considerations opposed it.

The motives underlying the trade with the French narrow down to one of two or to a combination of two. Undoubtedly, the personal gain accruing to those engaged in the trade, although it was not without risk, was the primary motive with the individual trader; but the tolerance and approval of the public needed a more general economic basis and this is to be found in the same reasons already advanced, making the trade between the West Indies and North America essential to each. To this may now be added the negative but strengthening circumstance that the general acceptance of the Molasses Act as a dead letter had destroyed the possibility that its evasion would cause any moral feeling of guilt or wrong-doing in the minds of the offenders or of the public.

Real Motives Underlying Contraband Trade

The unabashed manner in which the colonists persisted in their trade with the enemy served to bring the entire matter of illicit trade to the attention of the British people and government. Non-enforcement and general smuggling had caused the West Indies trade to take on features of a tolerated evil, and now it was the particular kind of smuggling that aided the enemy, which caused the British government to make almost the first serious effort to break up all kinds of illicit trade. A customs service which never had attempted to enforce the Molasses Act could not be whipped into an efficient working force when the crisis demanded it. The military arm, which was the first to feel vitally the crippling effect of the illegal trade with the enemy, **Recognition of Import- ance of Aid of Royal Navy to Customs Service** was the first to call to the assistance of the revenue officers the powerful British navy. Its co-operation seemed to strengthen the purpose of the regular custom-house officers, with the net result that the effort to collect the duties prescribed by the Molasses Act, with a view to a breaking up of the trade with the French, caused the revenue from molasses to increase from the average previous to 1755 of £259 to £1189 in 1761.[1]

This attempt at enforcement of the provisions of the Molasses Act caused the seizure of many vessels trading illegally and this, in turn, led to a conflict of authority between the vice-admiralty courts and the courts of common law. The former strove, generally speaking, to uphold the actions of the customs officers, and with them rested the legal right. The common law courts were influenced strongly by local prejudice [2]

Admiralty Courts vs. Common Law Courts

---

[1] G. L. Beer, *British Colonial Policy*, 115.

[2] Cf. Thomas Pownall on this point: "Under the third article, I fear experience can well say, how powerfully, even in courts, the influence of the leaders of party have been felt in matters between individuals. But in these popular governments, and where every executive officer is under a dependence for a temporary, wretched, and I had almost said, arbitrary support to the deputies of the people,—it will be no injustice to the frame of human nature, either in the person of the judges, of the juries, or even the popular lawyer to suggest, how little the crown, or the rights of government, when opposed to the spirit of democracy, or even to the passions of the populace, has to expect of that support, maintainence, and guardianship, which the courts are even by the constitution supposed to hold for the crown. Nor would it be any injustice to any of the colonies just to remark in this place, how difficult, if ever practicable it is, in any of their courts of common law to convict any person of a violation of the laws of trade, or in any matter of crown revenue. Some of our acts of parliament direct the prosecution and punishment of the breach of the laws of trade, to take its course in the courts of Vice-admiralty: And it has been thought by a very great practitioner . . . that there should be an advocate appointed to

and feeling and the desire to please those from whom the judges' salaries were received, —the people. A jury that would convict was difficult to find. Thus we read of the Collector at New York arguing even in 1739 that the case arising from the seizure of gunpowder and molasses, imported illegally from St. Eustatia, should be tried before the Admiralty Court instead of before the common law court, and apprehending the unlikelihood of securing a favorable verdict from "a Jury who perhaps are equally concerned in carrying on an illicit trade, and its hardly to be expected that they will find each other guilty."[1] This speaks eloquently of the general prevalence of illicit trading and the temper of the public mind concerning it. The admiralty courts themselves were not above suspicion as is witnessed by the complaints sent to

each court from Great Britain, who, having a salary independent of the people, should be directed and empowered to prosecute in that court, not only every one who was an offender, but also every officer of the customs, who through neglect, collusion, oppression, or any other breach of his trust became such." Thomas Pownall, *The Administration of the Colonies*, 4th ed., pp. 108 ff.

[1] A. B. Hart, *American History Told by Contemporaries*, Vol. II, No. 87, quoting " Documents relative to the Colonial History of the State of New York," VI, 154–155. It was the illegal importation of gunpowder, contrary to the Act of 1663, and the enforcement of that act, which seem to have interested the Collector most in this case.

General Amherst concerning the courts in South Carolina, New York, and Pennsylvania.[1]

So established, in fact, in public sentiment was the trade with the foreign West Indies, that as the war drew toward its close, promising the return to normal conditions, the attempts to collect the duties imposed by the Molasses Act appear even to have been relaxed.[2]

[1] Cf. G. L. Beer, *British Colonial Policy*, 126, notes 1, 2, 3, 4.
[2] G. L. Beer, *British Colonial Policy*, 230, and n. 3; cf. 116.

CHAPTER IV

POLITICAL SITUATION IN ENGLAND AND AMERICA

General
View of
Situation
as Revealed
by Contra-
band Trade
with French THE situation which existed in the customs service and the admiralty courts, which the prevalence of smuggling during the French War caused to be exposed, was hardly one to bring delight to the heart of the British government. The statement of Howard, a Rhode Island lawyer with Tory leanings, presents what may be considered as the British view. He said, "It is notorious, that smuggling * had well nigh become established in some of the colonies. Acts of parliament had been uniformly dispensed with by those whose duty it was to execute them; corruption * had almost grown into a system; courts of admiralty * became subject to mercantile influence; and the king's revenue sacrificed to the venality and perfidiousness of courts and officers."[1]

[1] A Letter from a Gentleman at Halifax, to his Friend in Rhode-Island, containing Remarks upon a Pamphlet, entitled, "The Rights of Colonies Examined." (Newport, 1765). Reprinted in Hart, *American History Told by Contemporaries*, II, sec. 139.

It was this state of things that the administrative measures of Grenville, described in the chapter following, were designed to reform. At the same time at which the discouraging facts in connection with the status and evasions of the Acts of Trade and Navigation, and especially of the Molasses Act, were brought into the limelight in England by the illegal trade with the French, the British Exchequer was confronted with a serious shortage in funds. Although the colonies had for the most part paid a proportionate amount of the enormous sum expended in their defense,[1] the maintenance of the vast domain, acquired at the cessation of hostilities, involved the annual expenditure of many more millions for which experience had taught the voluntary aid

British Need of Revenue

---

[1] Lord Sheffield gives the following items of expenditure by Great Britain on account of the American colonies,

By the war of 1739	£31,000,000
By the war of 1755	71,500,000
Total	£102,500,000

Doubling this amount by the £100,000,000 expended in the war of the Revolution, he adds, "And thus have we expended a larger sum in defending and retaining our Colonies, than the value of all the merchandise which we have ever sent them; we have, in a great measure, disbursed this enormous sum, to secure the possession of a country which yielded us no revenue, and whose commerce called for but £1,655,092 of the manufactures of Britain." *Appendix*, page 301.

of the colonies could not be depended upon. Revenue from some source was a necessity.

The Grenville Act of 1764 sought to raise this revenue largely from that part of the trade of the colonies which it was apparent was the most flourishing and which had been yielding practically no returns in duties. The "Sugar Act" amended the Molasses Act, imposing a new duty on refined sugar and lowering the duty on molasses and syrups.[1] As if to offset possible and expected resistance from the colonists, the use to which this revenue could be put was specifically provided. It was not to be used for the general expenses of the British Exchequer but only for the expenses in part of maintaining the military establishment in the colonies, while three years later the Townshend duties were to be devoted to those of administering justice and for the support of civil government in the colonies,

" Sugar Act "

Revenue Measures

---

[1] The duties imposed by the "Sugar Act" were, "For every hundred weight avoirdupois of such foreign white or clayed sugars, one pound, two shillings, over and above all other duties imposed by any former act of parliament." Upon molasses the act declared, "That in lieu and instead of the rate and duty imposed by the said act upon melasses and syrups, there shall, from and after ... (Sept. 29, 1764) be raised, levied, collected, and paid unto His Majesty, for and upon every gallon of melasses or syrups, ... the sum of three pence."

and any surplus could be legally used only for the support and protection of the colonies.[1]

To aggravate the situation, England was in an unsettled political condition over the same questions. The British farmer objected to bearing the expenses of a war waged in behalf of the untaxed colonists, who, by smuggling, had always eluded most of the possible duties. Add to the fact that the colonists were heavily in debt to the British merchants, the grievance that "The fact was notorious that by the evasion of the navigation laws and acts of trade, the colonists had escaped the restrictions intended by those laws, and at the same time had received bounties and drawbacks from the British Exchequer which enabled them to undersell the British merchants in the markets of Europe,"[2] and it is easy to appreciate the feelings of the one party in England. Fur-

Unsettled Political Situation in England

[1] The Sugar Act reads, "That all the Monies which shall arise by the several Rates and Duties herein before granted ... shall be entered separate and apart from all other Monies paid or payable to His Majesty ...; and shall be there reserved, to be, from time to time, disposed of by Parliament, towards defraying the necessary Expenses of defending, protecting, and securing, the British Colonies and Plantations in America."

[2] Mellen Chamberlain in J. Winsor, *Narrative and Critical History of America*, VI, 18.

thermore, as we have seen, the continuance of the late war on the part of France was made possible largely because of the goods and supplies delivered by the smuggling expeditions of the colonists.

The colonists and their sympathisers in England maintained that they were paying more than their share of the military and main-

Colonists' Objections to Revenue Measures

tenance expenses, on account of the vast amount of trade which they were obliged to throw to England, but expressed a willingness to aid further, provided such aid was voluntary. In England, the frequently changing cabinets were filled with men of divergent views. Pitt recognized the futility of an attempt by Parliament to place a fixed tax from without upon a people trained to believe such a procedure opposed to all natural laws.

Another great question loomed up before the two parties on either side of the sea,— that of the "prerogative." The Liberals were attempting to transfer the power of the prerogative from the Crown to Parliament. Now the Albany Congress in 1754 had admitted the fact that all property in unoccupied lands belonged to the King, not to the people or a

party, and that therefore the political relations were with the Crown,—"Not citizens
within the Realm, but subjects only of the
Crown." Franklin reasoned, "Sovereignty of
the Crown I understand. The sovereignty
of the British legislature out of Britain I do
not understand,"[1] and later, "America is not
part of the dominions of England but of the
King's dominion."[2] From the liberality of the
charters, granted always by the King, and
from the privileges usurped without contest
and enjoyed for such a long time that they
seemed almost as granted rights, the colonists
had built up a bulwark of rights and assumed
rights, the modification of which by Parliament invited vehement opposition. It is not
to be supposed, however, that the colonists
were any fonder of the "prerogative" as such
than were the Liberals in England: they simply appealed to it to escape Parliament;
against its exercise they objected as strongly
as did the anti-prerogative party in England.

The systems of government among the
American colonies and the character of the

The " Pre-
rogative "

[1] *Works*, IV, 208. [2] Ibid, IV, 284. Marginal notes of Franklin's
on English pamphlets.

people are elements which must be considered before we begin to inquire into the methods adopted to enforce the Sugar Act and the reception it received.

In considering either the material or political development of the mainland colonies of North America, it soon becomes manifest that it was the possible economic or financial returns which guided the course of the home country relative to establishing forms of government. Until the middle of the seventeenth century, the policy, if it may be called such, of the Crown was to give a free rein to those trading companies and individuals, which it had deputized for colonizing purposes. The settlements were divided into many provinces and lacked any semblance of unification. Save Virginia in 1624, it was not until 1680 that any of the colonies was organized under a definite royal government. When the governments took their final shape there was exhibited a wide variety in the forms; the semi-independent in New England, the closely checked proprietary in Maryland, the liberal proprietary in Pennsylvania, and the royal in most of the colonies.[1]

Looseness in Colonial Governments

[1] See C. McL. Andrews, *Colonial Self-Government.*

These different forms of government had, however, two elements in common. First, representation in some form was accorded to the people. Second, the influence of Parliament was completely overshadowed by that of the King. All charters were liberal. The possession of these privileges for several generations fixed in the minds of the colonists the idea that the privileges were natural rights and it was the attempts of succeeding ministries to make this representation of minimum value, coupled with the effort of one party to maintain the power of the King's prerogative and, of the other party, to increase the power of Parliament, that stirred up the spirit of unrest and defiance of the next ten years.

Points of Similarity in Forms of Government

In dealing with the North American colonies, moreover, England was facing a problem differing radically in many respects from any of its other colonial problems; and it was a problem which had no precedents for guidance. Previously, no colonies had attained either the extent or the importance of those in North America. Their natural resources made them of great advantage to the mother

Unique Character of the American Colonies

country and the colonists were quick to grasp this fact. The colonists themselves were, as a rule, above the average of settlers. The motives which caused them to leave the mother land were higher than the average. The adventurers were outnumbered by the seekers after religious and political liberty. England was dealing with a class of colonists more nearly on a plane with her own citizens. In the last third of the seventeenth century, Sir Josiah Child was able to write, "I am now to write of a People whose Frugality, Industry, and Temperance, and the happiness of whose Laws and Institutions, do promise to themselves long Life with a wonderful encrease of People, Riches, and Power."

G. L. Beer points out that "The movement toward independence dates from the very foundation of the colonies"[1] and gives as reasons that the New England settlements were not a result of natural expansion but were more of the nature of a schism or secession. The original characteristics of extreme individualism in the immigrants were strengthened by the isolation of the colonies. It was

Reasons Contributing to Development of Spirit of Independence

[1] G. L. Beer, *British Colonial Policy*, 161.

the policy of England to have the colonies bear their own administrative expenses, through appropriations from the colonial legislatures. Governors and judges were thus dependent on the people for their salaries and the colonists were early to learn that by the withholding of salaries they could exert a great influence over the actions of the officials. This not only made evasion of law easy but served to awaken the people to a fuller consciousness of the possibilities of gaining independence.

If it is true—and the facts seem to justify Beer's conclusions—that a spirit of independence was ever the underlying motive for all unrest in the colonies, it may be assumed that the colonists did not have any clear conception of it, and had they had, a sense of policy would have led them to keep expression of this spirit in the background. More was to be gained in every way by expressions of loyalty to England than by manifestations of a desire for independence. However great may have been the influences, some of which we have noted, that would tend to keep alive the spirit of independence, there was always the oppos- **Spirit of Independence Kept in the Background** ing fact of weight that powerful enemies of the colonies, as well as of England, were present in America. As long as Spain and France exercised any powerful influence in America, so long was it essential that the English colonies should remain under the nominal protection of England, for they were not strong enough to defend themselves and their shipping. The danger from the Spanish was the first to be eliminated and the French were finally disposed of in 1763.[1] Remaining in America as the only possible foes of the colonies were the Indians, and the danger from them was such as the settlers could overcome by their advantage in organized numbers and a superior civilization.

The first genuine political sentiment common to all the colonies appeared simultaneously with the passage of the Sugar Act in 1764, and the preparations to enforce it. The Molasses Act, practically vitiated by thirty years' constant, nearly reputable, almost legalized smuggling, was the occasion of nothing more than sporadic outbursts of in-

[1] For a full treatment of the results, political and social, of the French and Indian War, cf. G. E. Howard, "*Prelim. of the Revolution*," chap. i.

dignation, arising for the most part from those who were occasionally affected financially. The change to the Sugar Act which, if enforced, would be felt, directly or indirectly, by every citizen of every community, awakened a genuine protest based, it would seem, less on the burden of this tax itself than on the principle of taxation involved.

It is a mistake to assume that customs taxation in itself was an innovation to the colonists, as one might well imagine from the clamor which the acts of 1763 and 1764 aroused. Besides the Parliamentary plantation duty of 1673, and one or two others, the assemblies of the various colonies had from the start levied taxes and duties. No general or unified system could exist, but in practically all the colonies export and import duties and tonnage duties were levied. The tariff measures were usually adjusted to changing needs. A very thorough study of the commercial legislation of the colonies by A. A. Giesecke[1] reveals a mass of such measures the extent of which would lead to the conclusion that the colonists would have been accustomed to the payment

Earlier Acts of Self-Taxation by the Colonists

[1] A. A. Giesecke, *American Commercial Legislation before 1789.*

of all kinds of duties and taxes. Substantially all these measures were measures of self-taxation. The later effort of Parliament to enforce general revenue duties introduced new elements capable of arousing opposition.

Previous to 1763, the political clouds were such as might arise in the skies of any nation with colonies at a great distance and with inadequate means of communication. Unpopular governors met with disfavor, the signs of which no pains were taken to conceal. Colonial legislatures had their differences with their overlords. There existed then, as now, the hot-headed, excitable, and incendiary element in society, whose clamor was probably louder than their influence merited. The majority of the people would have been classified as Tories, for, as late as 1776, the number of Tories was estimated at about two-fifths of the entire population. What discontent existed previous to 1763 was local rather than general in character. No unity of purpose was evident among the different colonies and, in fact, they were not unified in any particular either of government or of sentiment. Even the

Political
Troubles
Local in
Character

Acts of Trade could provoke no unanimous protest, for provisions which offended one section were considered as beneficial by another, and restrictive measures in which were latent the means of arousing the most general disapprobation, remained unenforced and ineffective.

About 1756, "writs of assistance" began to be used in Massachusetts, and later in New Hampshire, by the customs officers to aid in their work against the smugglers. The writs were issued by the Superior Court and directed any officer or subject of the King to aid in the forcible search for contraband goods in any vessel, store-house, or private building. They were transferable general warrants extending during the reign of the sovereign, and returns were to be made to no officer or court. In England, this form of writ had been used since the reign of Charles II under act of Parliament, and it was issued by the Exchequer Court. By the Act of the 7th and 8th of William III its availability seemed to be extended to the colonies without the naming of any court of issue. The Massachusetts Assembly had given the same judicial authority

"Writs of Assistance"

to their Superior Court as that possessed by the Exchequer Court, and the Court overcame, if it had them, its scruples against

granting writs.

Upon the death of George II in 1760, all writs would expire within six months, and organized opposition was formed against the petitions to the Court praying for new writs. Mr. Gridley had charge of the case for the collectors and the government. A large part of his argument was consumed in attempting to prove the legality of the writs, to Hutchinson who was presiding at the hearing of the petition. Mr. Justice Gray, commenting on the legal aspects of the case, says, "A careful examination of the subject compels the conclusion that the decision of Hutchinson and his associates has been too strongly condemned as illegal." [1] The legal questions, however, concern us less, but sufficient consideration must be given them to make plain the fact that the granting of the writs had a legal basis. Of more relevance was Gridley's conclusion, "It is true the common privileges of Englishmen are taken away in this Case, but

[1] Quincy's *Reports*, 540.

even their privileges are not so in cases of Crime and fine. 'Tis the necessity of the Case and the benefit of the Revenue that justifies this Writ. * * * The necessity of having public taxes effectually * * collected is of infinitely greater moment to the whole, than the Liberty of any Individual."[1]

John Adams, in old age, wrote that Otis, for the people, began his famous argument with "A dissertation on the rights of man in a state of nature." "From individual independence he proceeded to association." "These principles and these rights were wrought into the English constitution, as fundamental laws." He "demonstrated that if the acts of trade were considered as revenue laws, they destroyed all our security of property, liberty, and life, every right of nature, and the English constitution and the charter of the province." "The Americans * * had connived at the distinction between external and internal taxes, and had submitted to the acts of trade as regulations of commerce, but never as taxation, or revenue laws." He showed that the acts of trade were "unjust,

James Otis's Alleged Arguments Against Writs

---

[1] Quincy's *Reports*, 481.

oppressive, and impracticable; that they never had been and never could be executed; that 'if the King of Great Britain in person were encamped on Boston Common, at the head of twenty thousand men, with all his navy on our coast, he would not be able to execute these laws. They would be resisted or eluded.'" In connection with the Molasses Act, "He asserted this act to be a revenue law, a taxation law, made by a foreign legislature, without our consent, and by a legislature who had no feeling for us, and whose interest prompted them to tax us to the quick."[1]   The general trend of Otis's speech is then summed up in Tudor's words, "He reproached the nation, parliament, and king with injustice, illiberality, ingratitude, and oppression in their conduct towards this country."[2]   A. B. Hart is of opinion that Otis's actual speech "marks the tone of public opinion in Massachusetts in 1761," and that it may be regarded "as the first in the chain of events which led directly and irresistibly to revolution and independence."[3]

[1,2] This and preceding quotations are from Tudor's *Life of James Otis*, Chap. VI.   But see criticism by C. F. Adams in Adams' *Works*, X, 362, n.; Gray in Quincy's *Reports*, p. 469, n.; and Ashley in *Surveys*, pp. 356 ff.

[3] A. B. Hart, *American History Leaflets*, No. 33, Introduction.

CHAPTER V

THE year 1763 marks the converging of the political and economic forces operative in America. We have endeavored to show that the English commercial system divides itself into two parts. The main structure, consisting of the enactments concerning the means of shipping, and the trade between America, England, and the other countries of the world, excepting the West Indies, was considered by the ruling powers and parties in England economically advantageous to England. It happened to be in active force during the critical period in American history: its inception antedated the formation of some of the colonies and its continuance did not cease with England's loss of her American possessions.[1] The natural products of England were less diversified than those of America; those of America were many and various. A

Main Body of Trade Laws Incapable of Arousing Universal Political Feeling

[1] See S. G. Fisher, *The Struggle for American Independence*, p. 68.

system which met with general favor in England because of its apparent aid to home industry could not be expected to arouse a similarly unanimous negative sentiment among the different colonial sections whose varied industries were variously affected, and it did not. Those acts of trade which were constructed with a certain degree of reciprocal feeling towards the colonies could be appreciated in some sections and meant nothing in others. The restrictions on the rights of the colonists to buy except in the British markets were not seriously felt as a grievance, because the effect of this portion of the laws was largely to legislate commerce into those channels into which economic necessity would have naturally forced it. We may eliminate, therefore, this main portion of the Acts of Trade and Navigation as a matrix for the development of any very strong or general spirit of independence, common to all the colonies.

Universal Effect of Molasses Act

The remaining part, the Molasses Act, based essentially on special favoritism to one party in interest, with all traces of mutual benefits omitted, would, if enforced, place all the colonies to a greater or less extent in a state of protest against the same inevitable result,—the ruin of a trade economically essential in some measure to each.

For thirty years the Molasses Act had remained practically unenforced. The time chosen to enforce it was the same at which the restraint on the desire for independence, Forces Converging in 1763 caused by the presence of France in America, was removed. It was the same time at which the attempt of Parliament to contest the prerogative, a purely political move in which, to preserve their charter privileges, the Americans had some interest on the side of the King, was especially urged in England. The occasion which called the old Molasses Act and subsequent Sugar Act into an active life was the need of revenue, so that at this otherwise very inopportune time there was involved another principle most obnoxious in every respect to every colonist at all times,—taxation. This last feature served as a flux to fuse together all those influences which had always tended towards each other in the composition of a revolutionary spirit.

That which followed the decision to raise a revenue by means of the Sugar Act is inti-

mately connected with the features of the
evasions of the Molasses Act previous to 1763.
Each of the new regulations passed to facilitate the execution of these revenue acts is
directly traceable to the fact that the great
extent of the smuggling, expecially during the
French War, showed only too clearly to the
British government just where weaknesses
lay and how they could best be remedied, and
the possibilities in revenue in which a strict
enforcement would result.

Immediately following the decision to enforce the Trade Acts and to use the duties as
Officers
of the Navy
Empowered
to Act as
Customs
Officials
revenue mediums, Grenville and his cabinet
became very active in having passed the necessary measures. It is of importance to note
that instructions to the governors were sent
by a Secretary of State or emanated from the
Treasury and not simply from the Board of
Trade, indicating the complete change in
purpose. The attempt to break up the illegal
trade with the French had made it manifest
that the most potent instrument which the
government could bring to bear against illegal
trade in general was the royal navy. The
Navigation Act of 1660 had given authority

to the officers of the navy to aid in its enforcement only in the case of vessels violating the
law restricting the carrying trade of the colonies to English or colonial ships. The civil
officers alone were empowered to enforce the
other provisions of that and succeeding acts.
To give the navy, then, the power to proceed
against all forms of illegal trade, it was enacted
in 1763 that officers of the navy should be
on the same footing as custom-house officers.
Special ships were also fitted out for the purpose of intercepting illegal trade.

The evident weaknesses in the custom-
house organization itself were also revealed by
the smuggling in the past years. The correct-
ing enactments were aimed at the most patent
of these. The connivance of the officials
having made possible much of the smuggling,
all discretionary powers were henceforth Reorgan-
denied to customs officers. They were for- ization of
Customs
bidden to accept as formerly the duty on Service
part of a cargo as payment for the whole, and
their salaries were established on a firmer
basis, diminishing the temptation for them to
resort to bribes. All coasting vessels, which,
although of small tonnage, could go to the

West Indies, had to get "sufferances" and take detailed "cockets" at each lading. This had not been demanded before and therefore those vessels most suitable for the smuggling trade had been free from such supervision. Those high in the customs service, who were wont to remain in England, were ordered to their posts and received strict instructions to do their utmost to prevent all forms of illegal trade, in order to obtain as great a revenue as possible. Jurisdiction in all cases arising from the Acts of Trade was given to the admiralty courts, sitting without juries. The governors of all the provinces were required to report on the state of trade in their dominions. In passing, we should notice that these reports asserted that violations of the Acts of Trade in general were infrequent and of small relative importance. The evasions of the Molasses Act were always excepted and in some of the reports were entirely omitted, the facts being too well known for restatement. To connect more closely the administrative officials with England, the Earl of Northumberland was appointed, in 1764, Vice-Admiral for all America, and William Spry, Judge of the Vice-Admiralty

Court for all America. Later, in 1768, Customs Commissioners for America, five with Burch and Hulton, entered on the scene. These were the essential changes made to bolster up the administration of the Trade Laws. The "writs of assistance" which we have seen were first used about 1756, were the most potent instruments to serve the rejuvenated collecting arm of the British Treasury. Their use and abuse were confined for the most part to cases against evaders of the molasses and sugar duties. Whether or not we agree with President Adams when he says, "I do say in the most solemn manner, that Mr. Otis's oration against writs of assistance, breathed into this nation the breath of life," the fact remains that what caused the extended use of the writs to be attempted was the smuggling in connection with the West Indies trade.

Continued Use of "Writs"

At the same time as the reduction on molasses, duty was laid on Madeira wines and certain French and Oriental manufactures. Revisions were also made in the drawback system which operated to the advantage of the home country. A blending of purposes is here discernible, indicating that the transition

Additional Revenue Measures

from a protective to a revenue basis was gradual and that commercial influences were still at work. But the effect of the revenue-producing measures was so much more important that to the colonists the change appeared abrupt and momentous.

The combined efforts of the royal navy, hitherto particularly effective, and of the re-organized customs service were not of sufficient strength to break up the contraband trade. Both the war vessels, and the sloops especially fitted out to break up the smuggling, were lightly esteemed by the colonists. One writer asserts that the colonists considered it "a sacred duty" to break the trade laws.[1] Exaggerated as this statement is, it contains an element of truth. Previous to 1763 motives of self-protection may have led the merchants to consider it a duty to smuggle in all the goods possible; after that date, a feeling of resentment at the principles of taxation involved may have led the populace to give moral and material support to the revenue-evading traders. This conjecture is confirmed by a study of the events attending the

Smuggling Too Strongly Entrenched to be Broken Up

[1] S. G. Fisher, *The Struggle for American Independence*, I, 51.

attempted enforcement of the Sugar Act. Violence to custom-house officers had previously been almost unknown, probably because of their willingness to gain popular favor through a lax administration of their offices. Now, however, appeared a change in the temper of the people, and this hostile temper was incensed more and more until the war resulted. Take, for instance, a few of the less well-known occurrences noted in Scharf & Westcott's "History of Philadelphia."[1]

In 1769, John Swift, a revenue officer, seized a cargo of Madeira wine, placing it in a store-house. During the night the wine was stolen by a band of citizens, who later stoned the collector's house. Although the owner returned the wine to the officers and some of the leaders of the riot were arrested, informers in the case were seized, pilloried, and tarred and feathered. Armed vessels were used by the officers but their operation was made difficult in that when seizures were made, the prizes were usually rescued by armed men who had no fear even in destroying the King's ships. Perhaps the most just cri-

Public Sentiment Favored Law Evasion

[1] Scharf & Westcott's *History of Philadelphia*, III, 1801 ff.

terion of the temper of the people is found
in the following extract from Bradford's
"Pennsylvania Journal" of October, 1773, in
connection with the appearance in Philadelphia of Eben Richardson, a treasury spy sent
from Boston. After describing the man, the
Journal suggested that "All lovers of Liberty
will make diligent search and having found
this bird of darkness will produce him tarred
and feathered at the Coffee-House, there to
expiate his sins against his country by a
public recantation."

The stories of cargoes seized for non-pay-
ment of duties and rescued by rioters in Philadelphia are duplicated in the histories of each
of the great sea-ports. Added incentives to
forcible protests were found in the brutality
of the revenue officers in their eagerness for
private gain. It was alleged that in one year
the collectors pocketed illegally £17,000, while
it was further alleged that vessels illegally
laden, were allowed purposely to leave port
so that they could later be brought back as
prizes.

The one indubitable feature of the protests
against the enforcement of the Trade Laws

Brutality
and Greed
of Revenue
Officers

is that those who continued to evade them received the moral support of the people as a whole. This support increased each year after 1763. At that date, long established trade customs, based on what were considered natural rights, formed the main argument in justifying the traders to continue as formerly. But the effort to raise a revenue from this indispensable commerce served to arouse every citizen and that which aroused them was not primarily the burden of tax itself but a realization that danger lurked in the new principle propounded. Thus a question of government in relation to commerce served to awaken a political consciousness which exerted an increasingly strong influence, culminating in 1776.

Commercial Grievances Superseded by Political Grievances

In importance, the commercial and economic sources of dissatisfaction steadily dwindled while the political forces which they had generated increased even more rapidly. In the great political protest caused by the Stamp Act (1765), by the Townshend Acts (1767), and by the subsequent governmental regulations of Parliament, the commercial element is almost entirely lacking. A complete reversal of tactics on the part of the

colonists is exhibited in the Non-importation
Agreements (1765 and 1767–1770). In view
of the duties, it might have been expected
that a great smuggling trade would have
grown up in those European commodities so
essential to the Americans. But as the importation of these articles would have sooner or
later benefited principally England, the colonists were led, from political motives, to agree
not to import those articles, which, from an
economic standpoint, would have been of
great advantage to them.

The burning of the *Gaspee* in Narragansett
Bay (1772), and the destruction of the tea in
Boston harbor (1773), were "applauded by
the whole continent" as the newspapers of
National the time had it. A national spirit was being
Spirit
Developed rapidly developed and it needed now only
the use of military force by the British to
inflame the national political feeling into a
militant national spirit, striving for independence. By the time of the Declaration of
Independence, the objections to the commercial system were forgotten and no reference
is made to them in the grievances except that
of "cutting off the trade of the whole world,"

probably referring to the Boston Port Bill, a punitive measure and not a part of commercial policy.

It is not within the scope of this essay to continue further in following the developments directly preceding the formal break between the American colonies and England. The active influence of commercial regulations and their evasions had ceased. The movement which they were instrumental in starting had acquired sufficient momentum to carry itself along independently of any additional initial impetus in the form of dissatisfaction with commercial situations. After the British government came to a realization of the futility of any attempt to raise a revenue by the methods hitherto employed, and lowered or removed many of the duties previously obnoxious,[1] it was evident that the time was past when such conciliatory measures could avail Too Late in checking the movement for entire independence. for Conciliatory Measures

At the beginning we stated that it would

[1] Against the protests of the British agricultural interests, great concessions were made to the colonists in the suspension or removal of the restrictions on the importations of grain, beef, pork, bacon, etc. 6 George III, 3; 7 Geo. III, 4; 8 Geo. III, 9; 10 Geo. III, 2.

be our purpose to establish the part which smuggling played in the elements contributing to the development of the spirit of independence. Briefly let us summarize our facts and Conclusions conclusions with this purpose distinctly in mind:—Lax administration and consequent universal evasion of governmental regulations designed to restrict that part of the colonial trade which economic reasons demanded should be free and unrestrained, permitted this trade—that with the foreign West Indies—to develop to such an extent and importance that interference with it would entail commercial disaster which the colonies could not withstand. When the Seven Years' War made it necessary for England to attempt to break up the trade because of the aid it gave to the French, the magnitude which it had attained, the inefficiency of the customs service, and the usefulness of the royal navy were revealed. When, at the close of the war, the need of funds was pressing in England, the great possibilities of revenue which would result from a strict enforcement of the Molasses Act, modified into the Sugar Act, led Great Britain to strike at the West Indies trade in particular. Thus, the form of smuggling most general at the outbreak of the Revolution,—almost the only one of any extent which could have been caused by considerations other than those of private greed,—a form of smuggling which had formerly been considered, by reason of long enjoyment, as almost legal trade, was now transformed, by the decision to enforce the Sugar Act, into smuggling in a very real sense.   This occurred at a time when the political forces incident upon the introduction of taxation measures and the removal of the danger from the French in America, directed the minds of the Americans towards independence.   In this coalescence of commercial grievances and the political grievances to which they contributed, the former were finally completely overshadowed by the latter, and smuggling must therefore be considered as an ultimate rather than as an immediate cause of the culmination of the spirit of independence—the American Revolution.

BIBLIOGRAPHY

The following bibliography represents a list of the works consulted in the preparation of this essay.

JOHN ADAMS, *Works.* 1850–1856.

C. McL. ANDREWS, *Colonial Self-Government* (American Nation Series). 1904.

JOHN ASHLEY, *Some Observations on a Direct Exportation of Sugar from the British Islands.* 1735.

W. J. ASHLEY, *Surveys, Historical and Economic.* 1900.

G. BANCROFT, *History of the United States.* 1882–1884.

G. L. BEER, *British Colonial Policy.* 1907.

G. L. BEER, *Commercial Policy of England towards the American Colonies.* 1893.

Sir F. BERNARD, *Select Letters on the Trade and Government of America.* 1764.

E. G. BOURNE, *Spain in America* (American Nation Series). 1904.

EDW. CHANNING and A. B. HART, *Guide to the Study of American History.* 1896.

EDW. CHANNING and A. B. HART, *American History Leaflets*, Numbers 19 and 33.

B. EDWARDS, *History of the British West Indies.* 1793.

S. G. FISHER, *The Struggle for American Independence.* 1908.

A. K. FISKE, *The West Indies.* 1899.

BENJ. FRANKLIN, *Works*, edition by Sparks, 1856.

A. A. GIESECKE, *American Commercial Legislation before 1789. University of Pennsylvania Studies.* 1910.

H. GRAY, *Writs of Assistance*, in *Quincy's Massachusetts Bay Reports.* 1865.

E. B. GREENE, *Provincial America* (American Nation Series). 1905.

A. B. HART, *American History told by Contemporaries*, 1897–1901.

G. E. HOWARD, *Preliminaries of the Revolution*, (American Nation Series). 1905.

MACDONALD, *Documentary Source Book of American History.* 1908

D. MACPHERSON, *Annals of Commerce.* 1805.

JAMES MADISON, *Works.* 1865.

G. R. MINOT, Continuation of the *History of the Province of Massachusetts Bay.* 1798–1803.

MONTESQUEIU, *The Spirit of the Laws,* 1748.

S. A. MORGAN, *Parliamentary Taxation.* 1911.

JAMES OTIS, *The Rights of th^ British Colonists Asserted and proved.* 1764.

TIMOTHY PITKIN, *Statistical View of the Commerce of the United States.* 1817.

T. POWNAL, *Administration of the Colonies.* 4th Edition, 1768.

SCHARF & WESTCOTT, *History of Philadelphia.* 1884.

LORD SHEFFIELD, *Observations on the Commerce of the American States.* 6th Edition, 1784.

ADAM SMITH, *The Wealth of Nations.* 3d Edition, 1784 (1st, 1776).

SPARKS, *Diplomatic Correspondence of the Revolution.* 1829–1830.

W. TUDOR, *Life of James Otis.* 1823

C. H. VANTYNE, *The American Revolution* (American Nation Series). 1905.

W. B. WEEDEN, *Economic and Social History of New England.* 1890.

J. WINSOR, *Narrative and Critical History of America.* 1884–1889.

Pennsylvania Archives. 1852–1907.

Documents Relative to the Colonial History of New York. 1853–1858.

Critical Essays on authorities and sources are found in the works of E. B. Greene, G. E. Howard, and Justin Winsor, noted above. A very complete list of Public Records and Laws, General Sources, General Histories and Monographs, most of which touch on this subject, is given by A. A. Giesecke in *American Commercial Legislation before 1789.*

INDEX

Act of 1660, 11f.; 82f.
Act of 1663, 12f.
Act of 1673, 73.
Act of 1696 (7th & 8th of William III), 8; 75.
Act of 1699, restricting woolen manufacture, 22.
Act of 1733. See molasses act.
Act of 1750, regarding iron, 16f.
Act of 1757, 49: 54.
Act of 1764. See sugar act.
Acts of trade. See specific acts just above, ch. II, *passim*, and 8ff.; 14f.; 27ff.; 33; 75; 77; 80; 84; 85; 88f.; evasions of, probably unimportant, 27ff,; feeling about, 75. See molasses act, and navigation acts.
Adams, John, on the export of fish, 39f.; account of Otis's speech by, 77f.; judgment of, of same, 85.
Albany Congress, on King's title to unoccupied land, 66.
Aliens, prohibition of, from trading in colonies, 14f.
Amherst, General, complaint of, regarding supplying of French, 50f.; regarding courts, 60f.
Ashley, John, on export of sugar, 37, n. 2.
Azores, wines from, 13,n.

Balance of trade, unfavorable, 35; 37; less unfavorable to Southern colonies, 41.

Bancroft, on revenue from America, 9; on bounties for naval stores, etc., 17; on West Indies, 45.
Barrels and hogsheads, materials for, 39.
Beer, on value of colonies, 10; 44; on tea consumption and smuggling, 30f.; work of, on extent of contraband trade, 54; opinion of, on "the movement toward independence," 70; 71.
Bernard, on corruption of customs officers, 47; on import of molasses, 47f.
Board of Trade and Plantations, 46; 82: report of, on colonial manufactures, 20.
Boston, distilleries at, 36.
Boston Port Bill, 91.
Bounties, 17; 65.
Bowsprits, 12, n.; 17.
Bradford's Journal, extract from, 88.
Brandy, 38.
Bribes, 83; 88. See connivance.
Burch, a customs commissioner, 85.

Carrying trade, confined by navigation acts, 14f.
Cattle, 20; 42, n.
Child, on American colonies, 20; on character of colonists, 70.
Coasting trade, exclusion of foreigners from, 14f.; vessels for, 83f.; regulations concerning, 84.

97